AF700836

PILOT'S HANDBOOK

FOR

MODEL YB-49 AIRPLANE

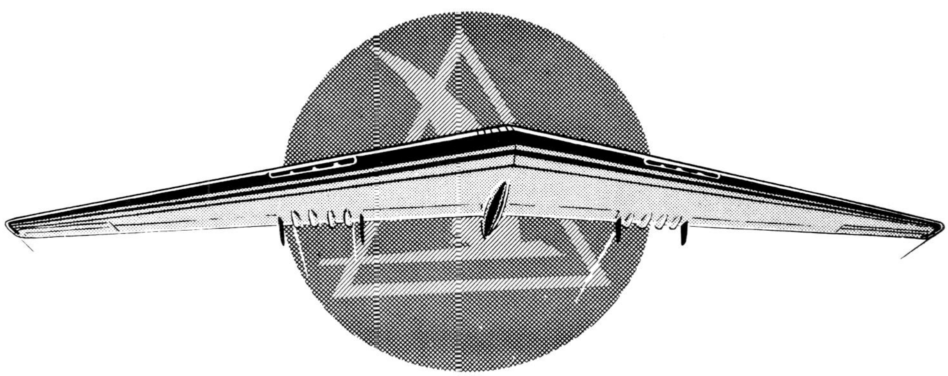

PREPARED BY NORTHROP AIRCRAFT, INC.
HAWTHORNE, CALIFORNIA

AIRCRAFT MANUAL SERIES

B-26 Martin Marauder
North American B-25 Mitchell Bomber
B-24 Liberator
B-17 Flying Fortress
Lockheed P-38 Lightning
Bell P-39 Airacobra
Curtiss P-40 Warhawk
Republic P-47 Thunderbolt
Northrop P-61 Black Widow
Bell P-63 Kingcobra
Chance Vought F4U Corsair
Grumman F6F Hellcat
Grumman FM2 Wildcat
F-82 Twin Mustang
Lockheed F-80 Shooting Star
Story of the Texan AT-6
Flying Wings of Northrop
Messerschmitt ME-262 Sturmvogel
DeHavilland Mosquito
Supermarine Spitfire
Hawker Hurricane
Ford Trimotor
Curtiss Standard JN4-D—Jenny
X-15 Research Airplane

TECHNICAL & REFERENCE MANUALS

Aircraft Detail Design Manual 2nd Ed.
Aircraft Hardware Standards Manual
  and Engineering Reference
Comprehensive Guide to Airfoil Sections
Handbook of Airfoil Sections for Light Aircraft
Helicopter Design and Data Manual
World War II International Aircraft
  Recognition Manual
Guide to Pre-1930 Aircraft Engines
Curtiss OX-5 Aeronautical Engine
J-3 Piper Cub Service Manual

AVIATION PUBLICATIONS
217 E. WASHINGTON ST.
P.O. BOX 357
APPLETON
WISCONSIN 54912-0357
U.S.A.

ISBN 0-87994-031-X

Litho in U.S.A. at Graphic Communications Center
with production by Badger Printing Division
Appleton, Wisconsin 54912

THE FLYING WINGS OF NORTHROP

by Leo J. Kohn

The airplane as we know it has been around for 70 years. Some are still being built in much the same manner as they have been for 50 years, and with relatively little difference in materials. Whatever progress has come about in the construction of airplanes has been accomplished mainly in the name of cost consciousness, and not necessarily only because of any contribution to an improved aerial vehicle.

In theory, at least, the main thrust of aeronautical science since the days of the Wright brothers has been mainly the reduction of a condition called "parasite drag." Parasite drag is drag created on an airplane by every item protruding from the airplane which does not directly contribute to lift. From the beginning, progress in aerodynamics can be traced to the enclosed fuselage, the single-bay interstrut wing layout, the transition from two wings to single high wing, then moving that wing to the low-wing position, folding the landing gear into the wing or fuselage to get it out of the slipstream, enclosing the engine with streamline cowling, making the wing full cantilever and thereby eliminating any supporting struts, and ultimately all-metal monocoque construction. Cost savings went hand in hand with drag reduction, and realizing a profit was the only reason anybody went into the business of building airplanes. Also, reducing drag meant increased fuel economy and performance for military and commercial operators. When we look over the modern array of aircraft we still find a good number which have not yet incorporated all of these "state-of-the-art" developments. Except for the development of the turbojet engine, which has to be considered the greatest single breakthrough in the development of the airplane, the airplane still remains substantially unchanged. One may argue then that the automobile also remains basically unchanged, still operating on four wheels as it has since its invention. However, the automobile requires the four wheels for its stable support, but the airplane requires only its wing for support in the air. All the rest of it can be considered of questionable necessity.

That was the thinking of John Knudsen Northrop, that the evolution of the form of the airplane had reached its ultimate and the next and apparently only logical step would be the all-wing aircraft, eliminating the fuselage and the tail surfaces. These tail surfaces have from the beginning provided the principal means of stabilizing and controlling the aircraft, and the fuselage was merely a structure to support these surfaces. Eventually the fuselage was enclosed, and even today a relatively large portion of the fuselage remains hollow and unused. Northrop was one of the few visionaries who actually wanted to produce a better airplane.

This requirement of tail surfaces at the extremity of a fuselage lever arm could not easily be compromised, for their complete removal would, in turn, present some new and interesting aerodynamic problems. Northrop, in his first attempt in 1929 toward an all-wing concept, had to accept the reality of controlling the aircraft according to conventional means. The wing by itself lacked all of the factors for the stability necessary for eliminating the tail surfaces. These control surfaces were carried on slim twin tail booms; however, he was making progress on the wing portion of the aircraft. The fuselage was gone, and both the two-man crew and the engine were placed within the 30-ft. 6-in. wing. At first, an extension drive to the propeller was used, but this was later changed to a direct-drive 90-hp Menasco A-4 engine.

The letting of federal air-mail contracts saw Northrop designing and building high-speed mail planes and passenger transports. On the basis of these designs, various military types were developed—the best of their day. The company was kept busy with its commercial and military contracts and became a subsidiary of Douglas Aircraft Corporation. There was no time to devote to development of the all-wing concept until Douglas absorbed the company in 1939. Northrop then organized the present company to concentrate on his approaches to aircraft design.

In July of 1940, the world's first successful all-wing airplane—the Northrop N-1M—became a reality. The functions of the elevator and aileron were combined into a single trailing-edge surface called an "elevon." Directional control was sought in a drag-producing device at the wing tips which would provide adequate yawing forces without affecting pitch or roll. During the course of wind-tunnel testing of models, 25 to 30 rudder configurations were tried before settling on the drooped wing tips with the drag surfaces.

The principal early problems with the N-1M related to the cooling of the two 65-hp Lycoming 0-145 engines which were buried completely within the wing. Because of the pusher arrangement, the engines did not benefit from slipstream cooling during taxiing, take-off, or climb. These cooling problems seriously handicapped the early flights, but these engines were later exchanged for larger 120-hp Franklins, and the design of cooling baffles was sufficiently improved so that repetitive sustained flights were easily accomplished. Otherwise, no serious difficulties were experienced in any flight attempt. Three-blade propellers were mounted on extension shafts and the airplane was nicknamed "Jeep".

The first flight of the N-1M, made by Vance Breese, was more or less an accident and occurred while taxiing over the Muroc Dry Lake bed at comparatively high speed. Breese struck an uneven spot and bounced into the air, resulting in a good controlled flight for several hundred yards before touching down again.

Moye Stephens took over the test program and made over 200 successful flights with the all-yellow N-1M. The craft provided for changes in planform, sweepback, dihedral, tip configuration, CG location, and control-surface arrangement, most of these being made between flights. Some of the adjustments felt better to the pilot than did others, but at no time was the airplane uncontrollable or unduly difficult to fly.

The N-1M was eventually given to the National Air and Space Museum where it is currently in storage and awaiting future display.

Once good sustained flight demonstrations of the N-1M could be made on schedule, the Army Air Corps began to take an active interest in the project. Generals Henry H. Arnold and Oliver P. Echols encouraged Northrop to investigate the application of the all-wing principle to large bomber aircraft. This was what John Northrop was looking for as there was no better way of demonstrating the merits of the concept than with a load-carrying, long-range, heavily armored aircraft. This resulted in the Northrop N-9M.

For this purpose, four N-9M's were built. These were 60-ft. scale models, employing improvements developed through the testing of the N-1M. "M" in the designation meant "mock-up" and, except for the powerplants and propeller arrangement, they duplicated the aerodynamic configuration of the XB-35. The N-9M was powered with two 275-hp Menasco engines, but the fourth N-9M was fitted with 300-hp powerplants. The first N-9M was flown on December 27, 1942 and, after about 30 hours of test flying, with an occasional observer on board, it crashed killing the pilot. None of the ground observers could see the crash, but most all evidence indicated a spin. This accident was a serious setback to the program and the engineers rechecked the spin characteristics. While spin recovery was quite different from conventional aircraft, it was good and no more troubles were encountered in this respect.

Development of the all-wing aircraft was a parallel effort to the design and manufacture of other military aircraft prior to and during World War II.

In 1943 Northrop designed and built the XP-56 *Dumbo,* a variation of the all-wing concept, it being a tailless pusher pursuit type. Only two were built, and used only for research purposes. The XP-56 was the first all-magnesium and all-welded aircraft, the first pusher to have contra-rotating propellers, and the first of its kind to have an aircooled engine completely submerged in the fuselage. As with the N-1M, it had its elevators and lateral controls on the trailing edge of the wing, but it had fixed vertical fins above and below the fuselage, to provide directional stability.

The next step in the development of the all-wing aircraft came with the MX-324 *Rocket Wing,* developed and completed in 1944 under the strictest secrecy, and not even revealed until early in 1947. This was America's first military rocket airplane, roughly a counterpart to Germany's successful efforts in that direction. The first flight, which was made in the presence of a few Northrop and Army Air Force representatives, occurred at Harper's Dry Lake near

Barstow, California on July 5, 1944. The MX-324 successfully employed a prone cockpit layout and new principles of rocket propulsion. It had a fixed faired tricycle landing gear, but some models were designed to take off and to land by means of a skid. Wing span was under 30 ft., and the prone position enabled the pilot to withstand high accelerations, but it also made possible a thinner airfoil section. The rocket motors were Aerojet XCAL-200 models, burning monoethylaniline fuel oxydized with red nitric acid.

Out of the MX-324 program came the XP-79B *Flying Ram*, the world's first jet-propelled all-wing aircraft and first prone-pilot fighter. The XP-79 and XP-79A were only engineering designs culminating in the single XP-79B, powered by two Westinghouse 19B turbojets of 1150 lbs. thrust each. It was literally a jet-powered battering ram, intended to dive on enemy bombers and "slice-off" their tail sections. The wings were fabricated of heavy magnesium plate to withstand the terrific ramming blows, while the pilot lay prone in order to raise his blackout threshold. The XP-79B was small but lethal, with a span of less than 38 ft. and length of 14 ft., while its gross weight was 8670 lbs. Its top speed was in excess of 500 mph, and directional control was accomplished through bellows-type rudders mounted on each wing tip. It was towed into the air in early test stages and, in this glider version, it came closest to the "ideal" all-wing craft with its original configuration displaying only a slight bulging of the wing leading edge at the center to accommodate the pilot.

Northrop further built the JB-1, a tiny glider built to test the efficiency of this type of design for flying bombs. It was less than 30 ft. in span. A Northrop test pilot flew this glider version in various experiments to prove its superiority over conventional types. Following these tests, a series of "buzz bombs" was built to the same pattern and designated JB-1A. These had no cockpit or canopy, as actual "buzz bombs" were pilotless. In the JB-1A, a warhead of nearly two tons was carried within the cast-magnesium inner section of the wing on each side of the single-resonance-duct jet engine which was carried on the centerline. Earlier development of the JB-1A employed twin-duct jet engines.

These years of experimentation and development proved that an all-wing aircraft had some distinct advantages over conventional types. Low drag and high lift were attained by reason that all exposed parts created lift and had little drag. An all-wing aircraft could carry any weight faster, farther, and more economically. The wings were simple and cost less to build since the fuselage and tail surfaces were eliminated, and the load was distributed over the span of the wing making heavily reinforced structures unnecessary. The machine took up less space in a hangar or parking area and was easier to service. It was also harder to spot on a radar screen.

Continuous experimentation and flight testing of the N-9M's led directly to the huge XB-35 bomber, the 13th successful tailless all-wing aircraft built by Northrop. For all practical purposes, the N-9M was a flying-scale model of the XB-35.

Early in World War II the United States had to think in terms of the eventuality of British defeat, and therefore a bomber was needed which possessed the capability of reaching Germany from the North American continent and return. The long-range XB-36 was already being planned for this intercontinental bomber role. However, thinking was that increasing the size of the bomber would only result in a larger aircraft in order to carry the larger engines required to carry the additional fuel required for the mission —

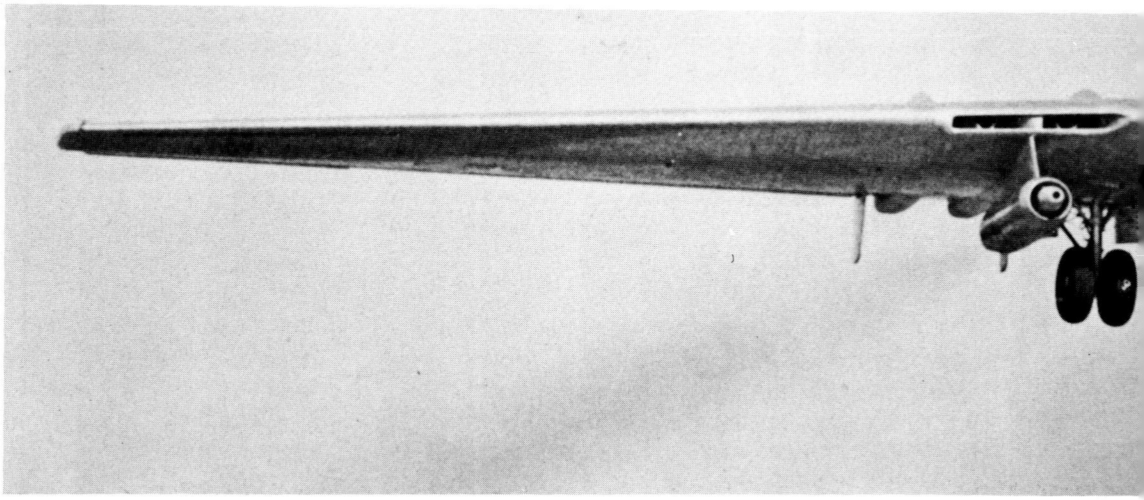

a viscious circle! Nothing was really to be gained from this approach, proven thoroughly with the experimental XB-15 and XB-19 bombers.

On the other hand, the full potential of the all-wing aircraft could only be realized in a very large size where everything could be housed in the thick wing. Army funding provided the resources needed by Northrop to develop this ultimate aircraft.

The Northrop plant at Hawthorne was fully committed to the production of the P-61 *Black Widow* and A-31 *Vengeance,* and the Glenn L. Martin Company was given a contract for the detail design and powerplant installation of the XB-35. Martin was also given a letter of intent for the production of 200 B-35's. The manufacture of the XB-35 was begun in early 1943 at Hawthorne.

Hardware and installation problems unique to the all-wing layout caused delay upon delay until well after the end of World War II. At the end of the war the letter of intent for 200 bombers was withdrawn. Meanwhile, engineers from the Otis Elevator Company were called in to assist in completing the structural design of the wing, a seemingly unlikely source of expertise to which the aeronautical engineers had to turn.

The XB-35 was ready on June 25, 1946, and the Northrop test team of Max Stanley and Fred Bretcher, along with Flight Engineer Orva H. Douglas, had the monster airborne for the first time in less than 3000 ft. The aircraft was immediately flown to Muroc Army Air Base in a flight that lasted 44 minutes and caused a sensation on its arrival. The ship performed according to expectations on this initial test and revealed no aerodynamic problems. This was well ahead of the first flight of the XB-36 which had been begun almost a year earlier.

Meanwhile, the N-9M's were used to train pilots for flying the XB-35. The XB-35 was AAF 42-13603, and the first and second YB-35's were AAF 42-38323 and AAF 42-102366 respectively. The Navy was supposed to get one, to be designated XB2T-1. Fifteen airplanes were built for the Army Air Force—the XB-35, and 14 YB-35 and YB-35A models. It was estimated that the B-35 would offer 25 percent increased efficiency over conventional bombers.

Normally, 8000 gals. of fuel were carried, but it had a maximum capacity of 18,000 gals. Its maximum bomb load consisted of 32 1600-lb. bombs, while its 20 .50-cal. machine guns were each supplied with 1000 rounds of ammunition. Four sighting stations controlled the operation of these guns. Defensive armament was never actually fitted on the XB-35.

From the very beginning the propellers were the singlemost source of grief for the XB-35. Even their delivery held up testing of the airplane and its No. 1 engine was fitted with three-blade propellers for engine and taxi tests. The propeller governors proved troublesome and prevented any early flights of substantial duration. On one of its first flights it made a satisfactory landing with both engines shut down on one side because of total loss of propeller control. The contra-rotating propellers gave so much trouble that they were eventually removed and replaced by large four-blade paddle propellers. Because of overlap and interference with the next propeller and consequent vibration, the XB-35 could not be flown as fast as with the previous propellers. More man-hours were spent on problems associated with standard and off-the-shelf hardware than because of the radical design of the aircraft.

With the weight of the fuselage and tail eliminated, the total empty weight of the XB-35 amounted to

only about 40 percent of its allowable maximum gross weight. With all loads carried inside the wing, the structure could be built lighter and more efficient, as more of the load distribution could be achieved over the entire wing area rather than concentrated largely in the fuselage as with a conventional aircraft. The wing was built as a single unit with a chord length at the centerline of 37 ft. 6 in. The landing gear, fitted with dual main wheels, was electrically operated.

The XB-35 had a loading of 40 lbs./sq. ft. while the Boeing B-29 had a 75-lbs./sq. ft. wing loading. This light wing loading had advantages with respect to rate of climb and ceiling. However, the additional wing area penalizes an all-wing aircraft in obtaining its maximum efficiency. To attain the same landing speed as a conventional aircraft, the "all-wing" had to land at 35-percent less weight, but this deficiency would be experienced only under conditions requiring use of maximum lift coefficient such as take-off, landing and stall. With the trail-edge controls neutral, the "all-wing" would possess all of the advantages previously outlined.

Northrop had still not reached his ultimate objective of a smooth exterior surface without protuberances of any sort. So far, the "wings" had included canopies, propeller shafts, gun turrets, and other exterior shapes through practical necessity.

A wing employing either a symmetrical airfoil section or one incorporating reflex camber at the trailing edge and without dihedral possesses all aerodynamic characteristics necessary for both longitudinal and lateral stability. To provide trim control, a segment of the wing trailing edge is hinged to act as an elevator. This is one of the major drawbacks of the "all-wing" for the movement of this surface changes the camber of the attached airfoil, and therefore affects wing lift, drag, and pitching moment. When this surface is moved up it reduces wing camber and therefore wing lift, reducing the wing's maximum lift coefficient from 20 to 40 percent. This results in take-

off, stall, and landing speeds considerably higher than with a conventional aircraft. Consequently, the wing must incorporate more wing area for a particular gross weight than with other aircraft.

Wing twist was included to prevent tip stall. Slots were used near the tip which were sealed in high-speed conditions and opened in low-speed flight to increase the stalling angle of the tip region.

The lever arm of the wing for elevator action was short, and power-actuated controls provided entirely adequate pitching control. The wing's CG was located far enough ahead of the center of aerodynamic balance to give pitching stability full comparable to that of conventional aircraft, particularly since shifts in load distribution occur mostly in a span-wise direction limiting necessary fore and aft CG travel to a fraction of that experienced in conventional aircraft. The N-1M tried drooped wing tips for stability, but these were later found to be unnecessary.

An unsolved problem of the "all-wing" is directional stability which demands an external surface if the same flying qualities as conventional aircraft were to be obtained. Use of wing sweepback provides some weathercock stability but not enough for satisfactory handling characteristics. With the B-35, the propeller-shaft housings and side forces of the propellers provided most of the required fin area. Lack of vertical surfaces on an all-wing aircraft made it difficult for the pilot to judge when a side-slip was taking place. The pilot's ability to feel these forces is essential for formation flying, steadiness on bombing runs, and for accurate gunnery.

Without the huge vertical surfaces on most conventional aircraft, the static yawing ability of the "all-wing" was reduced. But, because the wing does not suffer drag increases due to yawed flight, and whereas large vertical tails could in many cases actually be undersirable for dynamic stability, the wing again retains lateral characteristics fully comparable to conventional aircraft.

Directional control was obtained with hydraulic rudders located at the tips—flaps opening both up and down simultaneously and setting up a balanced drag. However, normal turns could be accomplished easily by elevon alone.

A total of 15 piston-engine B-35's were completed, but the B-36 was already entering squadron service as the last piston-engine strategic bomber. All the thinking and engineering was pointed toward jet power, and it appeared that the B-35 was a natural for jets and would provide the ultimate speed, range, and bomb-carrying ability. The Air Force ordered 30 jet-powered versions for experimental purposes, to be designated the B-49.

The most powerful jet engines available in 1945 were rated at only 3750 lbs. thrust, and eight were required to provide the required performance. The jet engines were considered better for the all-wing aircraft in keeping with the cleanliness of the design.

Basically, the YB-49 was a jet version of the XB-35, and flew for the first time in October, 1947. The first YB-49, AAF 42-102367, was off and flying in only 3500 ft. on its maiden flight from Hawthorne to Muroc. At over 100 tons and powered by the eight General Electric J35 engines developing a total of 32,000 lbs. thrust, it was the largest jet bomber at the time and the world's most powerful airplane. Two were completed, converted from the propeller-driven B-35's.

The YB-49 carried a crew of 13 – pilot, co-pilot, navigator, radio operator, bombardier, flight engineer, and gunner plus six reserve crewmen for relief work

XB-35 is first of Northrop's giant wings. It is powered with four 3,000-h.p. Pratt & Whitney pusher engines. Empty weight is 89,000 pounds but plane can operate at 209,000 pounds. Wing span is 172 feet. Contra-props have given repeated trouble. YB-49 is a jet version.

on long missions. Yet, it had many performance advantages usually found in nimble fighters. The biggest surprise was its climbing ability. Test pilots Stanley and Bretcher sometimes found it necessary to throttle back on the take-off climb because the ship accelerated so rapidly, and the danger of gear-down operational speed being exceeded before the gear could be retracted was an alarming presence. The landing gear itself consisted of four main wheels 5 ft. 6 in. in diameter and a single 4-ft. 8-in. nose wheel, the same as on the B-35.

The YB-49 used flat-plate separators on either side of the turbo-jet banks to prevent spanwise flow of the boundary layer. These fences extended completely around the wing trailing edge and forward almost to the leading edge. Four vertical fins were an integral part of these separators, extending above and below the wing trailing edge. These separators comprised only four percent of the wing area, and helped to distinguish the YB-49 from the B-35. Actually, they substituted for the propeller-extension fairings and propeller side forces of the B-35.

Conversion of ten of the remaining 13 YB-35's to eight-jet power was not to make them into YB-49's but into RB-35B's instead, signifying a modification to a basic airplane rather than an entirely new model. One of the remaining three airplanes was to be used as a static-test ship.

The United States Air Force requirements for a strategic reconnaissance airplane were kicked around more than any other category in the post-war years. The first competition was between the Hughes F-11 and Republic XR-12, with Republic getting the nod for its four-engine airplane. A contract was worked out for 20 R-12's, but a Senate investigation by Bennett Myers, Hughes and Brewster hit the front pages and the R-12 contract was placed in the "Pending" file at Wright Field.

In 1948 the Northrop "all-wing" was chosen to fill this gap and so Northrop was given a letter of intent for the 30 RB-49 reconnaissance planes. Northrop planned assembly of the first RB-49A at Hawthorne, with the remaining 29 to be produced by Consolidated-Vultee in its huge Fort Worth, Texas plant, right alongside the B-36 production.

However, the RB-49 program was washed out when it became apparent that considerable redesign would be required before it could go into production. Cancellation of the RB-49 contract was intended to release $300 million for a new quantity of B-36 and RB-36 bombers, and to modify existing B-50 bombers, to put a long-range striking force into combat readiness as soon as possible.

Northrop believed that the modification of the ten piston-engine B-35's to jet power was not affected by the RB-49 cancellation, although modification authority was supplemental to the RB-49 contract.

The first YB-49, in the meantime, had disintegrated in flight on June 5, 1948 near Muroc, killing its five-man crew. Its design limits were exceeded in a test dive. The crew included three Air Force test pilots and two civilians, one of the Air Force pilots being 30-year-old Capt. Glenn Edwards, and Muroc was eventually renamed Edwards Air Force Base in his honor.

In February, 1949, the second YB-49 flew non-stop for 2258 miles from Edwards AFB to Washington, D.C. for participation in the USAF Air Progress Demonstration. The flight was made at 511.2 mph, over 100 mph faster than the much revered B-36. It later flew with a full simulated bomb load at 382 mph for 3458 miles.

During the USAF Demonstration, President Harry Truman toured the interior of the YB-49 before the flight demonstration and was greatly impressed with what he saw. Upon climbing down the ladder he was overheard to comment to Air Force Secretary Stuart Symington that if it was up to him he "would buy it." Symington, in turn, was heard to ask "How many?," but Truman's response was not heard.

A month or so later, this same YB-49 was destroyed in a landing accident.

After cancellation of the RB-49 order, the Air Force was still interested and wanted to convert one of the ten B-35's to jet power for further evaluation. For this conversion, Northrop projected its own 10,000-lb. thrust *Turbodyne* turboprop engine, along with four General Electric J37 turbojet engines rated at 5000 lbs. thrust each for installation in the new YRB-49A. General Motors' Aeroproducts Division was building the propellers for the *Turbodynes.* This, too, was changed, and in 1949 the ninth YB-35 became the YRB-49A-NO, powered instead by six Allison J35-A-19 engines rated at 5600 lbs. each — four in the wing, and two in pods suspended below the wing. Completely in opposition to the purity of the all-wing concept, the two engines were underslung to make room for internal fuel capacity. It would seem that it would have been more logical to keep all six engines inside and carry the extra fuel in external tanks. Nevertheless, the YRB-49A had a range of over 9000 miles. Its empty weight was 88,500 lbs. and gross weight was 206,000 lbs. The airplane, which first flew on May 4, 1950, was tested thoroughly but development of the "all-wing" ended with it.

An 80-passenger airline version was created by

Jerry Fairbanks Products of Hollywood and might have evolved if the RB-49 had gone into production. However, the conservative airlines would not chance trying to place in service an unorthodox aircraft no matter how efficient and profitable it might prove. Had the "all-wing" been procured in large numbers as a bomber, Northrop would then have had an airplane easily converted into an airliner, already accepted and proven as a bomber and therefore much easier to sell to the traveling public.

The 23-year quest of John K. Northrop approached quite close to his goal but he never quite reached it. The last obstacle of providing directional stability on the jet version with no stabilizing fins or fences was still to be overcome.

A great backlog of flying experience on the YB-35's and YB-49's showed that excellent turns could be made without rudder and that, in general, these planes were far more maneuverable than their conventional contemporaries.

All non-load-carrying dead-weight items such as the tail and fuselage were eliminated from the net weight. Fuel and other load items spread out in the wing relieved bending stresses, while in conventional aircraft many of these items were concentrated on the centerline and increased stresses.

The "all-wing" achieved performance advantages from a combination of improved lift/drag ratio and a greater ratio of loaded to minimum weight. At higher cruising speeds, for which jet and turboprop powerplants are best suited, the lift/drag ratio for the all-wing aircraft was undeniably superior.

Had it not been for political and budgetary considerations, commercial air travel today might have been much different.

Leo J. Kohn

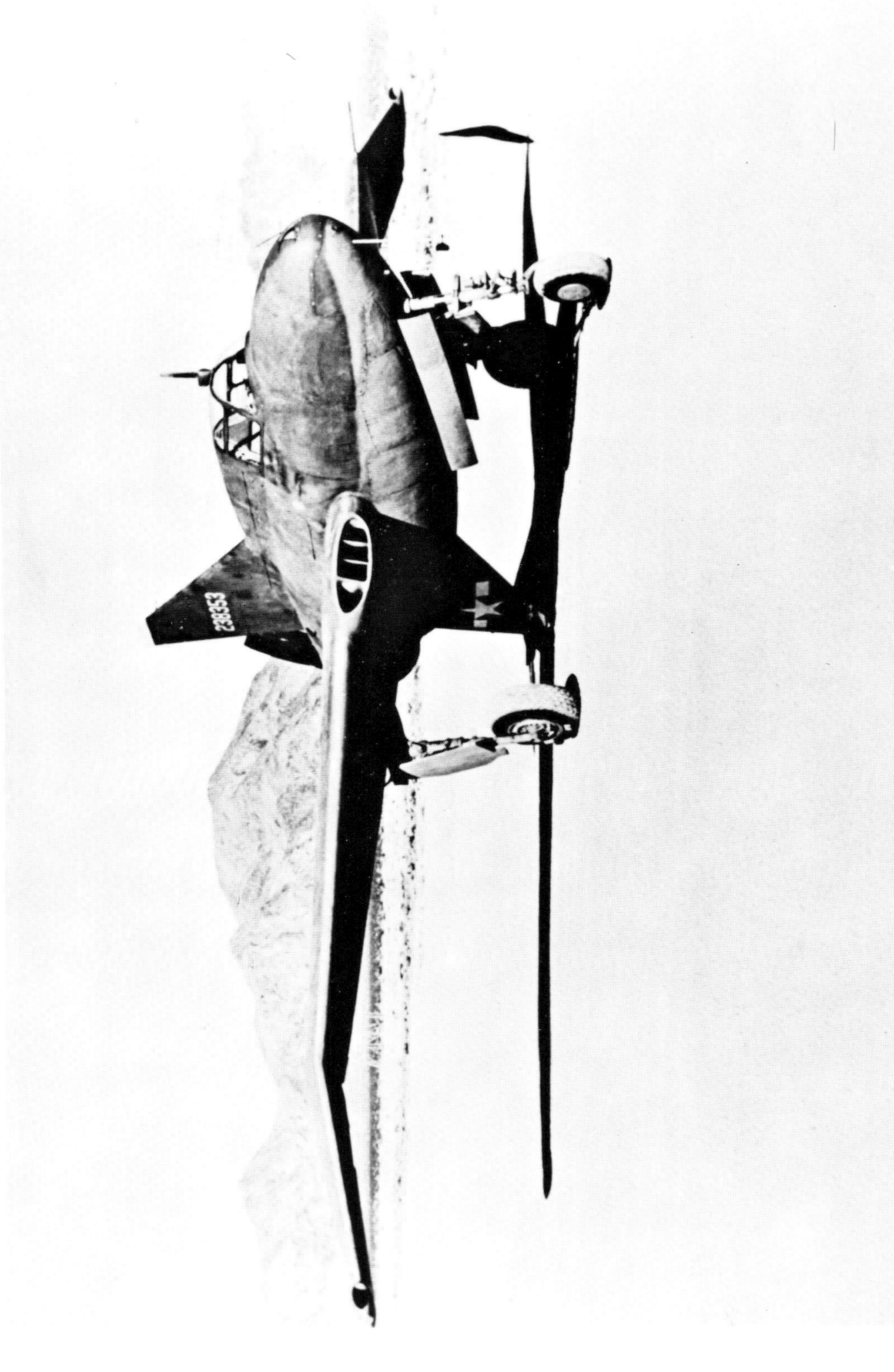
238353

2364 - 061 NORTHROP
N1-M

Northrop, XP-79A

Published under joint authority of the Commanding General, Army Air Forces, and the Chief of the Bureau of Aeronautics.

Commanding Officers will be responsible for bringing this Technical Order to the attention of all pilots cleared for operation of the subject aircraft as well as those undergoing Transition Flying Training as contemplated in AAF Regulation 50-16.

Appendix I of this publication shall not be carried on missions where there is a reasonable chance of its falling into the hands of an unfriendly nation.

SECTION I

DESCRIPTION

1-1. AIRPLANE.

1-2. GENERAL.

1-3. The Northrop YB-49 airplane is a turbo-jet propelled flying wing, designed for high altitude, long range, heavy bombardment missions. It is powered by eight J-35-A-5 engines; grouped four in each wing. The airplane has a wing span of 172 feet, a length of 52 feet, and height of 15 feet. The weight empty is approximately 89,000 pounds and the design gross weight and maximum alternate weight is 213,500 pounds.

1-4. CREW NACELLE.

1-5. The crew nacelle is located at the center of the wing and is divided into three parts, exclusive of a tail cone; the forward section containing the flight crew, the crew's quarters having provisions for a relief flight crew, and the aft gunner's station. (See figure 1-2.) The normal crew consists of a pilot, copilot, flight engineer, radio operator, navigator, and bombardier. Space is also provided for two gunners. The complete crew nacelle is pressurized, and personnel are free to move throughout the nacelle while in flight.

1-6. ARMAMENT.

1-7. The airplane has been designed to contain eight bomb bays, however only six are available in this airplane; three on each side of the crew nacelle (see figure 1-2). All gunnery equipment has been omitted on this airplane.

1-8. ELECTRICAL SYSTEMS.

1-9. GENERAL.

1-10. This airplane utilizes both alternating and direct current to operate most of its equipment and controls. Two auxiliary power units furnish 208 volts, 400 cycle, 3-phase alternating current. Direct current is supplied by two motor-generators that are operated by ac power. Alternating current circuits are protected from overload by limiters (fuses). The direct current circuits are protected by circuit breakers, automatic reset circuit breakers, and limiters (see figure 1-3). Principal ac and dc distribution circuits are wired in multiple with different wire routings which provide an additional safety feature.

1-11. A.P.U. SYSTEM.

1-12. GENERAL.- The ac power supply is derived from two 37.5 KVA, 208v, 3-phase, 400 cycle auxiliary power units. The units, hereafter referred to as A.P.U.'s are Franklin engine-driven alternator units installed in bomb bays 3 and 6. One 165 US gallon fuel tank is installed in No. 5 bomb bay to supply fuel to both A.P.U.'s. (See figure 1-6.) Two external dc-operated booster pumps are installed adjacent to the fuel tank which assure proper delivery of fuel to the A.P.U.'s. A solenoid-operated valve permits cross-feed-operation of the A.P.U.'s in the event of a booster pump failure. The tank is accessible from within the bomb bay. The A.P.U.'s operate on 91 octane fuel, Specification AN-F-48. Each A.P.U. is equipped with an integral oil sump containing 9 quarts of Grade 1065, Specification AN-0-8 oil. The A.P.U.'s are serviced from within their respective bomb bays. Alternating current power leads from each A.P.U. connect into a sectionalizing panel, through a circuit breaker, in the aft end of the A.P.U. bomb bay. Direct take-offs from these sectionalizing panels supply some motor-operated actuators in the inner wings. Power is led from these same panels to a ring bus in the crew nacelle. (See figure 1-4.) From the ring bus, power is distributed to electrical panels throughout the airplane where take-offs are made to various motors and actuators. Power is also routed from the ring bus to a transformer panel where it is stepped down to

No.	Item	Qty
1	FUEL FILLER	(12)
2	OIL TANK FILLER	(8)
3	MAIN LANDING GEAR AIR BOTTLE BUNGEE	(2)
4	D.C. MOTOR GENERATORS (IN MAIN GEAR WELL)	(2)
5	STOWED COVERS & LOOSE EQUIPMENT	
6	AUXILIARY POWER UNIT	(2)
7	AUXILIARY POWER UNIT FUEL TANK	(1)
8	PORTABLE OXYGEN CYLINDER	(2)
9	BEVERAGE JUG	(3)
10	OXYGEN FILLER PLUG	
11	CREW ENTRANCE HATCH	
12	BOMB BAY ESCAPE HATCH	
13	D.C. & A.C. EXTERNAL POWER RECEPTACLES	
14	ENTRANCE LADDER	
15	LAVATORY	
16	RADIO OPERATOR'S STATION	
17	BATTERY (IN NOSE GEAR WELL)	(1)
18	NOSE LANDING GEAR DOORS EMERGENCY BUNGEE AIR BOTTLE	(2)
19	FWD & UPPER ESCAPE HATCHES	(2)
20	EMERGENCY BRAKE AIR BOTTLE	(1)
21	GROUND CREW INTERPHONE	(1)
22	STEERING & BRAKE HYDRAULIC RESERVOIR FILLER	(1)
23	STEERING & BRAKE ACCUMULATOR & PRESSURE GAGE	(1)
24	BOMBARDIER'S KNEE PAD	
25	CO-PILOT'S STATION	
26	PILOT'S STATION	
27	NAVIGATOR'S STATION	
28	FLIGHT ENGINEER'S STATION	
29	HYDRAULIC RESERVOIR FILLER	(4)
30	NOSE GEAR BUNGEE	(1)
31	DC EXTERNAL STARTER POWER RECEPTACLES	(2)

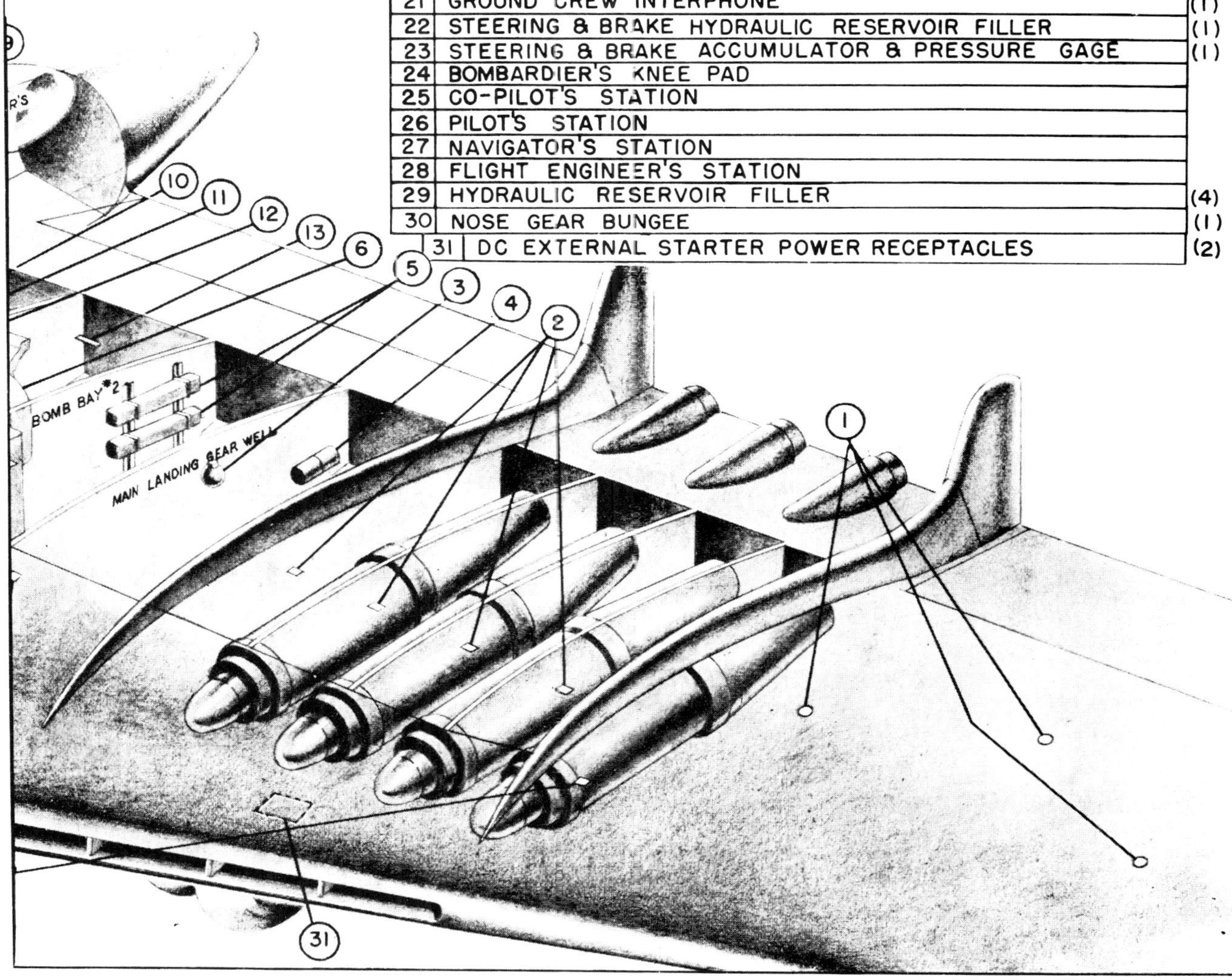

Figure 1-2. General Arrangement Diagram

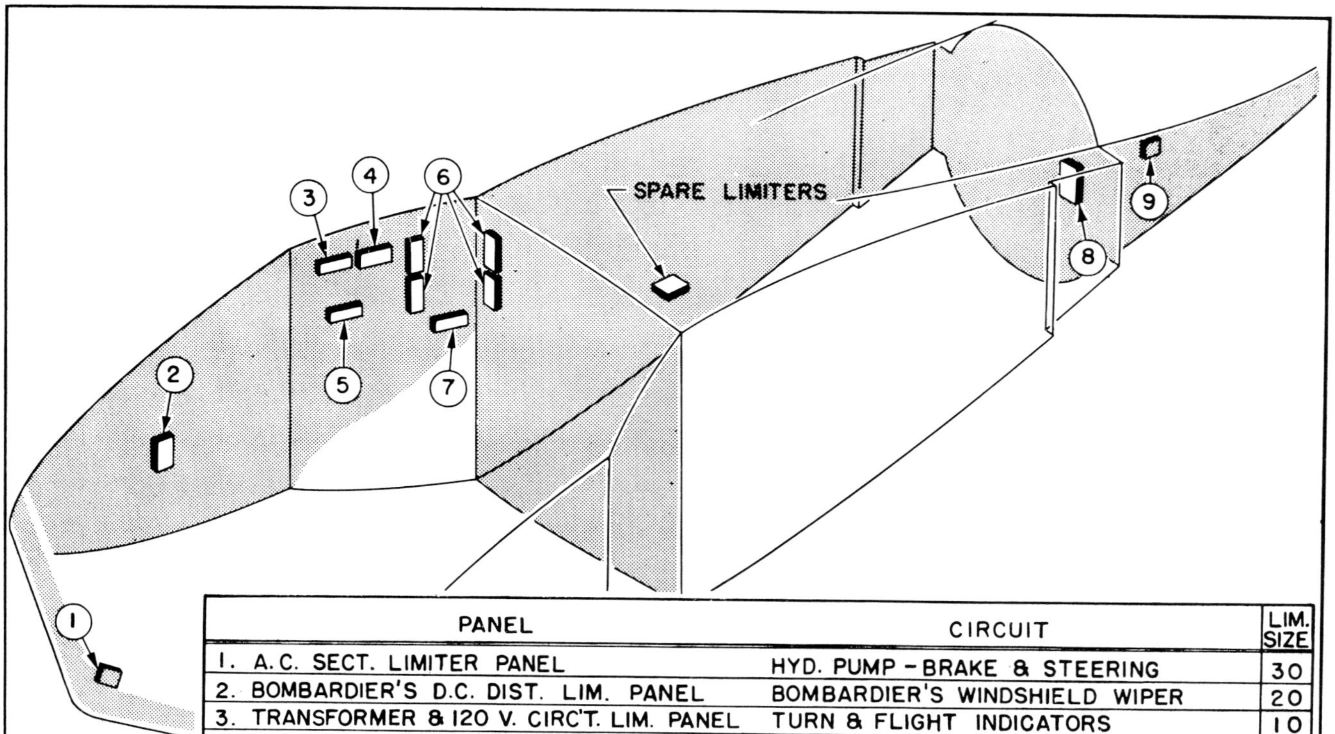

PANEL	CIRCUIT	LIM. SIZE
1. A.C. SECT. LIMITER PANEL	HYD. PUMP - BRAKE & STEERING	30
2. BOMBARDIER'S D.C. DIST. LIM. PANEL	BOMBARDIER'S WINDSHIELD WIPER	20
3. TRANSFORMER & 120 V. CIRC'T. LIM. PANEL	TURN & FLIGHT INDICATORS	10
	PITOT & CONTROL BELLOWS HEATERS	20
	BATTERY HEATER	20
	RADIO COMPASS	10
4. AFT. CREW NACELLE LIMITER PANEL	AFT CREW NACELLE	40
5. GROUND POWER LIMITER PANEL	EXTERNAL POWER	50
6. A.C. DIST. LIMITER PANEL	A.C. DISTRIBUTION	50
7. NOSE GEAR LIMITER PANEL	NOSE GEAR DOOR MOTOR	30
	NOSE GEAR ACTUATOR MOTOR	30
8. LANDING FLAP RELAY LIMITER PANEL	HEATED FLYING SUITS	30
9. AFT C.N. D.C. LIMITER PANEL	LANDING FLAP CONTROL	30

Figure 1-3. Location of Limiters

furnish low voltage ac for the operation of such equipment as the 115v gyro compass and the 30v suit heater controls. Burned-out limiters, located in the crew nacelle, can be replaced in flight by spare limiters that are carried in a loose equipment stowage bag located in the crew quarters. (See 5 figure 1-2 and figure 1-3.)

1-13. A.P.U. ENGINE CONTROLS.

1-14. GENERAL.- A control panel (see figure 1-5) installed at the engineer's station provides the engineer with control of the A.P.U.'s and ac power.

1-15. A.P.U. FUEL PUMP AND CROSS-FEED VALVE SWITCHES. (See figure 1-5.)- These two switches have "FUEL PUMP," "OFF," and "CROSS-FEED" positions. In the "FUEL PUMP" position, the switches operate the fuel booster pumps and open the fuel valves permitting fuel to flow to the A.P.U.'s. The "OFF" position, closes the fuel valves and stops the fuel pumps. The "CROSS-FEED" position stops the fuel pump, closes the respective fuel valve and opens the cross-feed valve. (See figure 1-6.)

1-16. A.P.U. FUEL SYSTEM SWITCH. (See figure 1-5.)- This switch furnishes dc power for the operation of the fuel booster pumps and fuel control valves.

1-17. A.P.U. LOW FUEL PRESSURE WARNING LIGHTS. (See figure 1-5.)- One light is furnished for each A.P.U. The lights will come on at any time that the fuel pressure at the carburetor drops to 7 psi. (Normal carburetor fuel pressure is 10 psi.)

1-18. A.P.U. PRIMER SWITCHES. (See figure 1-5.)- These switches operate solenoid valves which permit fuel to enter the intake lines. The fuel booster pumps must be operating in order to furnish fuel pressure for priming.

1-19. A.P.U. MAGNETO SWITCHES. (See figure 1-5.)- Each A.P.U. is equipped with dual ignition controlled by "ON-OFF" switches.

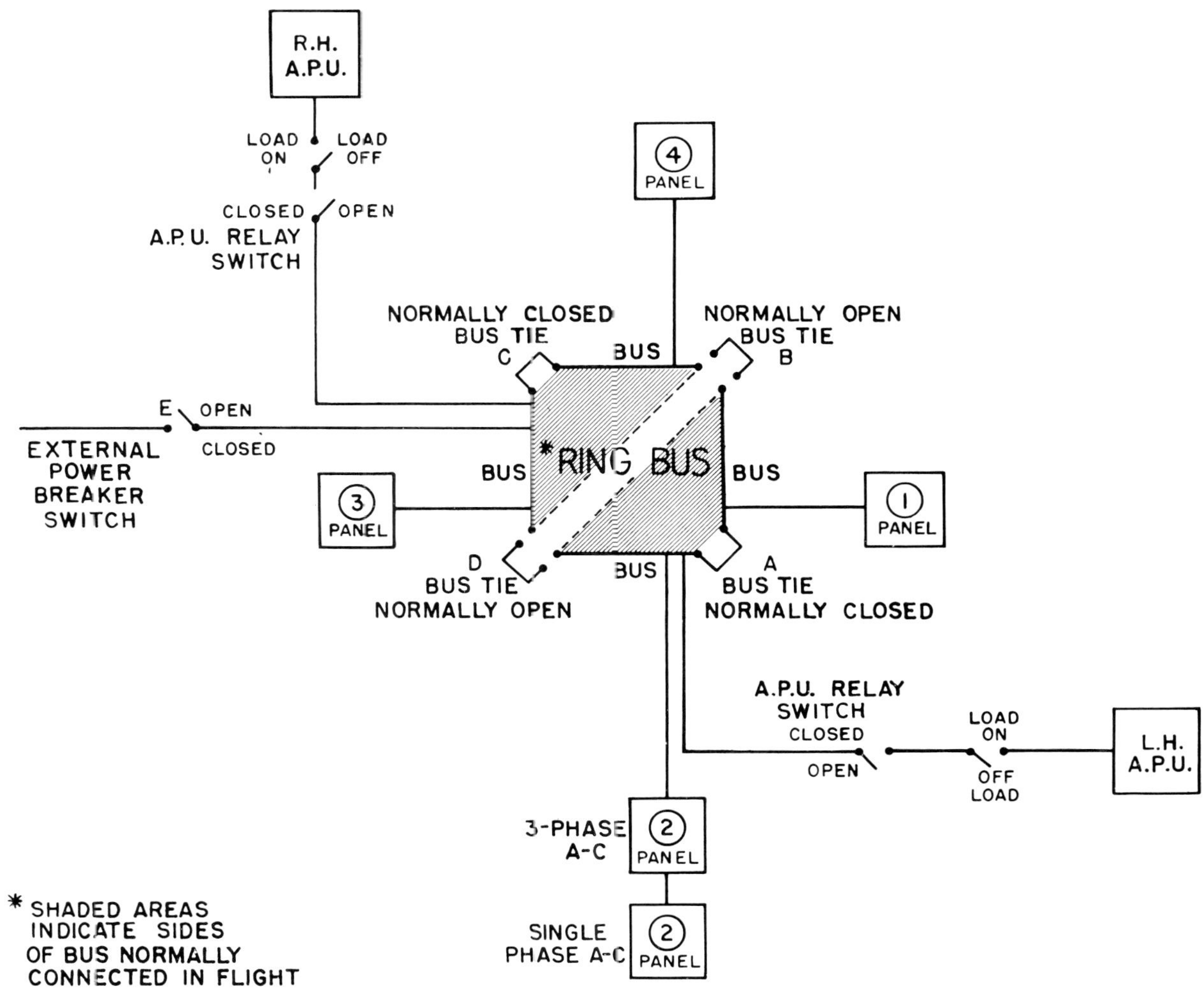

#1 PANEL
LH Trim Flap
5, 6, 7 Aux. Tank Pumps & Shut-Off Fuel Valves
1, 2 Engine Pumps (4)
1 Main Tank Fuel Shut-Off Valve
3, 4 Eng. Fwd. Pumps
LH Emergency Manifold Valve

#2 PANEL - 3-PHASE AC
BB 2, 3 Fuel Tank Pumps & Fuel Shut-Off Valves
BB 2, 3, 4 Door Open & Close Motors
3, 4 Eng. Aft Pumps
2 Main Tank Fuel Shut-Off Valve
LH Cross Feed Valve
LH Landing Gear & Gear Door
LH Motor Generator
Landing Flap Motors

#2 PANEL - SINGLE-PHASE
Radio Compass
Flux Gate Compass
Suit Heaters
Cabin Air Shut-Off Valves
Emergency Ram Air
Bomb Station Test Indicator Lights
Magnetic Compass Light
Driftmeter
Battery Heater
Auto Pilot
Pitot & Control Force Bellows Heater
A.P.U. Cooling
Ignition
Position & Formation Lights
Turn Indicators & Artificial Horizon
Heat Detectors

#3 PANEL
RH Motor Generator
RH Landing Gear & Door Motors
BB 6, 7 Pumps & Fuel Shut-Off Valves
BB 5, 6, 7 Door Open & Close Motors
RH Cross Feed Valve
3 Main Tank Fuel Shut-Off Valve
5, 6 Eng. Aft Pumps

#4 PANEL
RH Trim Flap Motor
Main & Aux. Nose Brake & Steering Hydraulic Pumps
Nose Gear & Gear Door Motors
7, 8 Eng. Pumps
4 Main Tank Fuel Shut-Off Valves
RH Emergency Manifold Valve
8, 9, 10 Aux. Tanks Pumps & Fuel Shut-Off Valves
5, 6 Engine Forward Pumps

Figure 1-4. AC Power System - Schematic

Figure 1-5. AC Control Panel

A green ignition light is installed above each magneto switch to indicate the operating condition of that circuit.

1-20. A.P.U. STARTER SWITCHES. (See figure 1-5.)- The starter switches are spring-loaded to the off position. They operate direct cranking starters with dc power.

1-21. A.P.U. SPEED CONTROL SWITCHES. (See figure 1-5.)- A.P.U. engine speeds are regulated between idle and full speed by spring-loaded switches which operate dc motor-driven governors. The governors control the throttles and act to maintain the selected speed of the A.P.U.'s. Indicator lights next to each switch show the idle or full speed operation of the A.P.U.'s and the dual tachometers register the actual rpm of the units. For further pertinent information regarding the use of these switches refer to paragraph 1-31.

1-22. A.P.U. COOLING AIR VALVE SWITCHES. (See 17 figure 1-12.)- Air for cooling and pressurizing purposes is ducted from the crew nacelle to each A.P.U. A fan that is integral with each unit expells this air through a duct that leads to an opening in each upper wing surface. A cooling flap is installed in both ducts so that the air flow can be regulated for cooling of the A.P.U.'s. A dual-indicating cylinder head temperature gage for the A.P.U.'s is located on the engineer's instrument panel. (See 14 figure 1-12.)

1-23. A.P.U. OIL TEMPERATURE SWITCH. (See figure 1-5.)- This switch turns the dc power "ON" and "OFF" for the operation of the OIL TEMP. indicators that are installed on the ac control panel.

1-24. A.P.U. OIL TEMP. INDICATORS AND LOW OIL PRESSURE WARNING LIGHTS. (See figure 1-5.)- An oil temperature indicator is provided for each A.P.U. There are two LOW OIL PRESS. lights (red) on the panel that light when the oil pressure drops below normal.

1-25. EXTERNAL POWER SYSTEM.

1-26. GENERAL.- Ac and dc external power receptacles are provided for ground operation of the airplane's equipment and starting of the engines (see 13, figure 1-2). The receptacles are located under a hinged cover located in the lower left wing surface just aft of No. 4 bomb bay. Ac external power is routed to one side of the ring bus through a dc operated contactor controlled by a spring-loaded switch on the ac control panel (see figure 1-5). This makes it necessary to have a dc power source, either the airplane's battery or external power, connected into the system before ac external power can be supplied to the ring bus.

1-27. EXTERNAL POWER RELAY SWITCH AND INDICATOR LIGHT. (See figure 1-5.)- This is a spring-loaded switch with "ON" and

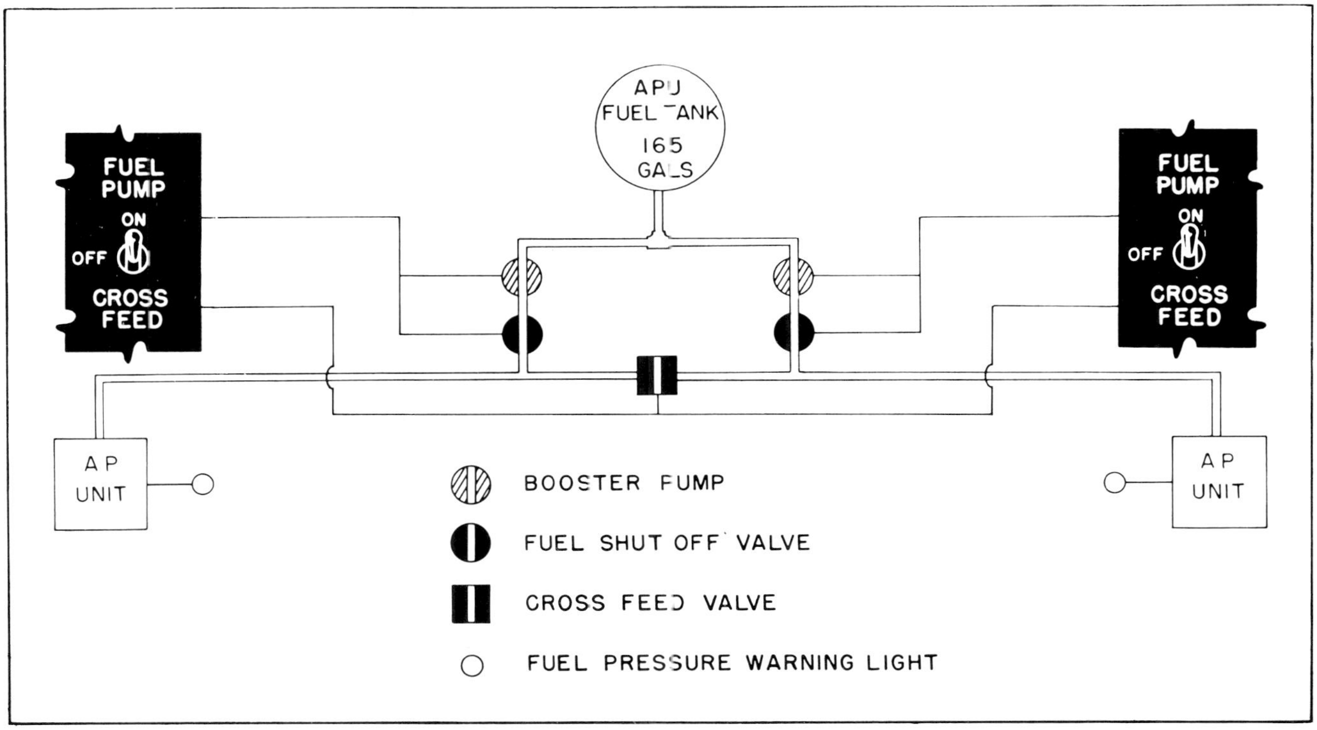

Figure 1-6. A.P.U. Fuel System

"OFF" positions. It controls a dc operated contactor to open or close the external power circuit to the ring bus. When this switch is "ON" an amber light, E, at the top of the panel will be on.

1-28. CIRCUIT BREAKER-RING BUS EXT. PWR. (See figure 1-5.)- This switch-type circuit breaker turns "ON" and "OFF" and protects the dc power circuit for the operation of the ring bus relays and the external power contactor.

1-29. ALTERNATOR CONTROL SYSTEM.

1-30. GENERAL.- The alternator controls are located on the ac control panel. (See figure 1-5.)

1-31. A.P.U. SPEED CONTROL SWITCHES. (See figure 1-5.)- The A.P.U. speed control switches regulate the speed of the A.P.U.'s and consequently the frequency (cycles) of the alternating current. (See paragraph 1-21.)

1-32. EXCITER FIELD SWITCHES. (See figure 1-5.)- Power output of an alternator is dependent upon its field being excited by direct current. This exciter current is supplied by a generator built into the alternator. The exciter current flow for each alternator is turned "ON" and "OFF" by a spring-loaded EXCITER FIELD switch. Holding a switch to the "OFF" position will cut the exciter current and therefore discontinue the output of the alternator.

1-33. A.P.U. RELAY SWITCHES. (See figure 1-5.)- These two spring-loaded switches operate relays to connect the A.P.U.'s into the ac distribution system. They are actually safety switches that must be used in conjunction with the LOAD ON switches in order to connect the units into the ring bus.

1-34. PARALLEL-NON PARALLEL SWITCH.- This switch is not used.

1-35. LOAD ON SWITCHES. (See figure 1-5.)- The two LOAD ON switches are used to place the units on the "line." i.e. to connect them into the ac distribution system.

1-36. LOAD OFF SWITCHES. (See figure 1-5.)- The two spring-loaded LOAD OFF switches are used to disconnect the A.P.U.'s from the distribution system.

1-37. PARALLELING LIGHTS.- These lights are not used. They are intended for use with parallel operation of the A.P.U.'s.

1-38. VOLTAGE CONTROL RHEOSTAT KNOBS. (See figure 1-5.)- These knobs provide means of adjusting the output voltages of the A.P.U.'s by regulating the exciter field current.

1-39. VOLTS AC INDICATORS. (See figure 1-5.)- One indicator is used with each A.P.U. The indicators constantly register the voltages of their respective units.

1-40. KW OR KVAR INDICATORS. (See figure 1-5.)- One indicator is used with each

A.P.U. These indicators show the amount of power in kilowatts (KW) used. KVAR readings cannot be taken.

1-41. AC AMPERE INDICATORS. (See figure 1-5.)- One ac ampere indicator is provided for each A.P.U. to show the amperes being used.

1-42. CYCLES INDICATORS. (See figure 1-5.)- The cycle indicators register the frequency at which each A.P.U. is operating.

1-43. BUS TIE SYSTEM.

1-44. GENERAL.- The power output of each A.P.U. is fed into a different segment of the ring bus. (See figure 1-4.) RING BUS RELAY switches are provided for connecting the ring bus segments together for parallel operation of both alternators or for operation of the complete airplane ac system by one alternator.

1-45. RING BUS RELAY SWITCHES AND INDICATOR LIGHTS. (See figure 1-5.)- The four RING BUS RELAY switches are lettered A through D. When a bus tie is off, a red light at the top of the panel for that bus tie will be on.

1-46. DIRECT CURRENT POWER SYSTEM.

1-47. GENERAL.- Power for dc uses is supplied by two ac-operated motor-generator-converter units and a 24-volt battery. (See figures 1-7 and 1-8.) For normal operations the battery is connected into the dc power system which permits the motor-generators to maintain the battery charge. An ac-operated heater is provided for the battery. In addition, the starter-generators on No. 4 and No. 5 engines are utilized for an auxiliary dc power source which may be used in the event of failure of the motor-generator units.

1-48. BATTERY.

1-49. GENERAL.- A 24-volt, 17 ampere-hour battery is located in the nose-wheel well. The battery is not intended for continued use in operation of dc equipment and whenever possible an external dc power source should be used when the motor-generators are not operating.

1-50. BATTERY CONTROL SWITCHES. (See figure 1-7.)- There are two battery control switches; one on the pilots' pedestal and one on the engineer's upper electrical control panel.

NOTE

The switches are wired in series, so both must be "ON" to connect the battery into the dc system.

1-51. BATTERY HEATER SWITCH.- (See figure 1-10.)- This two-position switch is used to control an ac heater which supplies heat to the battery.

1-52. EXTERNAL POWER SYSTEM.

1-53. DC EXTERNAL POWER RECEPTACLES. (See 13 figure 1-2.)- In order to conserve the airplane's battery, an external power source of 24-volts should be used on the ground when the motor-generators are not operating. A dc external power receptacle is located next to the ac receptacle in the lower surface of the left wing. There are no controls for the external power. Two dc engine starter receptacles on each side of the airplane are used to supply the starters with external power. (See 31 figure 1-2.) Each pair of receptacles is bussed together. This source of power is not connected into the airplane's dc system. When starting the engines a type C-16 power unit and two 12v jet-type batteries must be used to supply the 28v power for the starters on each side of the airplane. The batteries are connected together in series and in parallel with the two motor-generators contained in the C-16 power unit. Two power cables from the power unit must be plugged into the two receptacles that are located side-by-side.

1-54. MOTOR-GENERATOR SYSTEM.

1-55. GENERAL.- There are two ac-operated, 28-volt, 200-ampere, motor-generators in the airplane, identified as RH and LH. All controls and indicators for the motor-generators are located on a dc control panel. (See figure 1-8.)

1-56. MOTOR-GENERATOR CONTROL SWITCHES.- (See figure 1-8.)- A two-position, switch-type circuit breaker with "ON-OFF" positions is provided for each generator.

1-57. DIRECT CURRENT VOLTAGE RHEOSTAT CONTROL KNOBS. (See figure 1-8.)- A voltage rheostat control knob is provided for each motor-generator. They are located under a hinged cover on the edge of the dc control panel.

1-58. DIRECT CURRENT VOLTAGE SELECTOR SWITCH. (See figure 1-8.)- A multiple-position switch is provided for selecting each generator or the bus of both generators so that a voltage reading may be had on the single VOLTS DC indicator.

1-59. DIRECT CURRENT INDICATORS. (See figure 1-8.)- A single voltage indicator is provided for use with both generators, and one ampere indicator is provided for each generator.

1-59A. STARTER-GENERATOR SYSTEM.

1-59B. GENERAL.- Numbers 4 and 5 engines are equipped with starter-generators each having an output of 28v and 400 amperes.

WARNING

To prevent overloading the airplane's wiring system, not more than a 50% load should be placed on each starter-generator.

Normally these generators are not used, but if the A.P.U.'s should fail resulting in a failure of the motor-generator units, the starter-generators may be used to provide dc power for unlimited operation of dc equipment. Starter-generator controls are installed on a panel to the engineer's right. (See 7 figure 1-9.)

1-59C. STARTER-GENERATOR CONTROL SWITCHES. (See figure 1-8A.)- A two-position "ON-OFF" switch which ties the generator into the airplane's dc system is provided for each starter-generator.

1-59D. STARTER-GENERATOR VOLTMETER AND SELECTOR SWITCH. (See figure 1-8A.)- One two-position selector switch is provided to permit a voltage reading of either generator on the single dc voltmeter.

1-59E. STARTER-GENERATOR VOLTAGE RHEOSTAT CONTROL KNOBS. (See figure 1-8A.)- A rheostat control knob is provided to adjust the voltage of each starter-generator. The knobs are located under the hinged cover on the panel.

1-59F. STARTER-GENERATOR AMMETERS. (See figure 1-8A.)- There are two ammeters marked LOAD. They indicate the load in per cent that is being drawn from the starter-generators.

1-60. HYDRAULIC SYSTEMS.

1-61. GENERAL.

1-62. Five high-pressure hydraulic systems are used on this airplane. Four of the systems, termed the Power Boost Systems, furnish power for the operation of the primary flight control surfaces. Ground test connections are provided for each system, next to the reservoirs. (See 29 figure 1-2 and 10 figure 1-11.) The outboard connections are accessible through an access door in the lower wing surfaces and the inboard connections can be reached through an opening in the forward end of each main gear wheel well. The other system provides power for the operation of the main gear brakes and the steerable nose wheel.

1-63. HYDRAULIC POWER BOOST SYSTEMS.

1-64. GENERAL.- There are four separate and independent hydraulic power boost systems used on this airplane. (See figure 1-11.) Each system provides 2000 psi hydraulic pressure. Each engine drives one hydraulic pump and the pumps are connected in pairs. The outboard systems operate the outboard actuators for the rudders and elevons, and the wing slot door actuators for their side of the airplane. The inboard systems

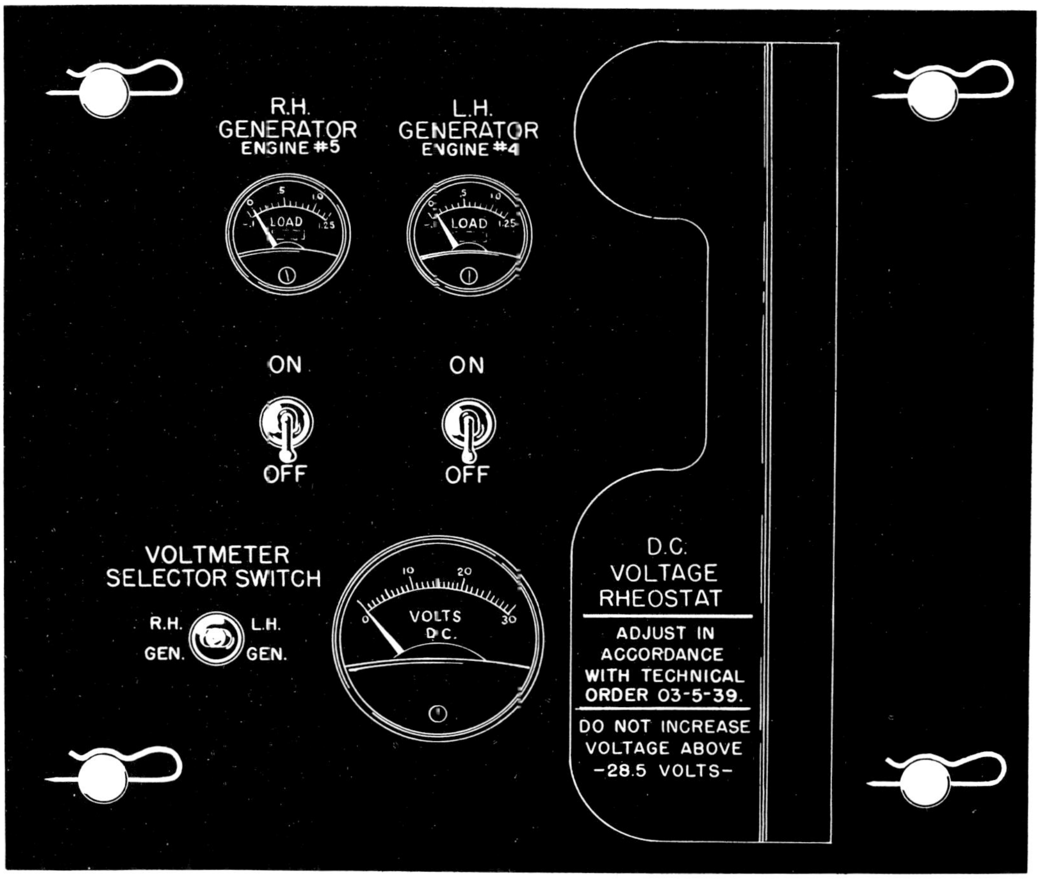

Figure 1-8A Starter-Generator Control Panel

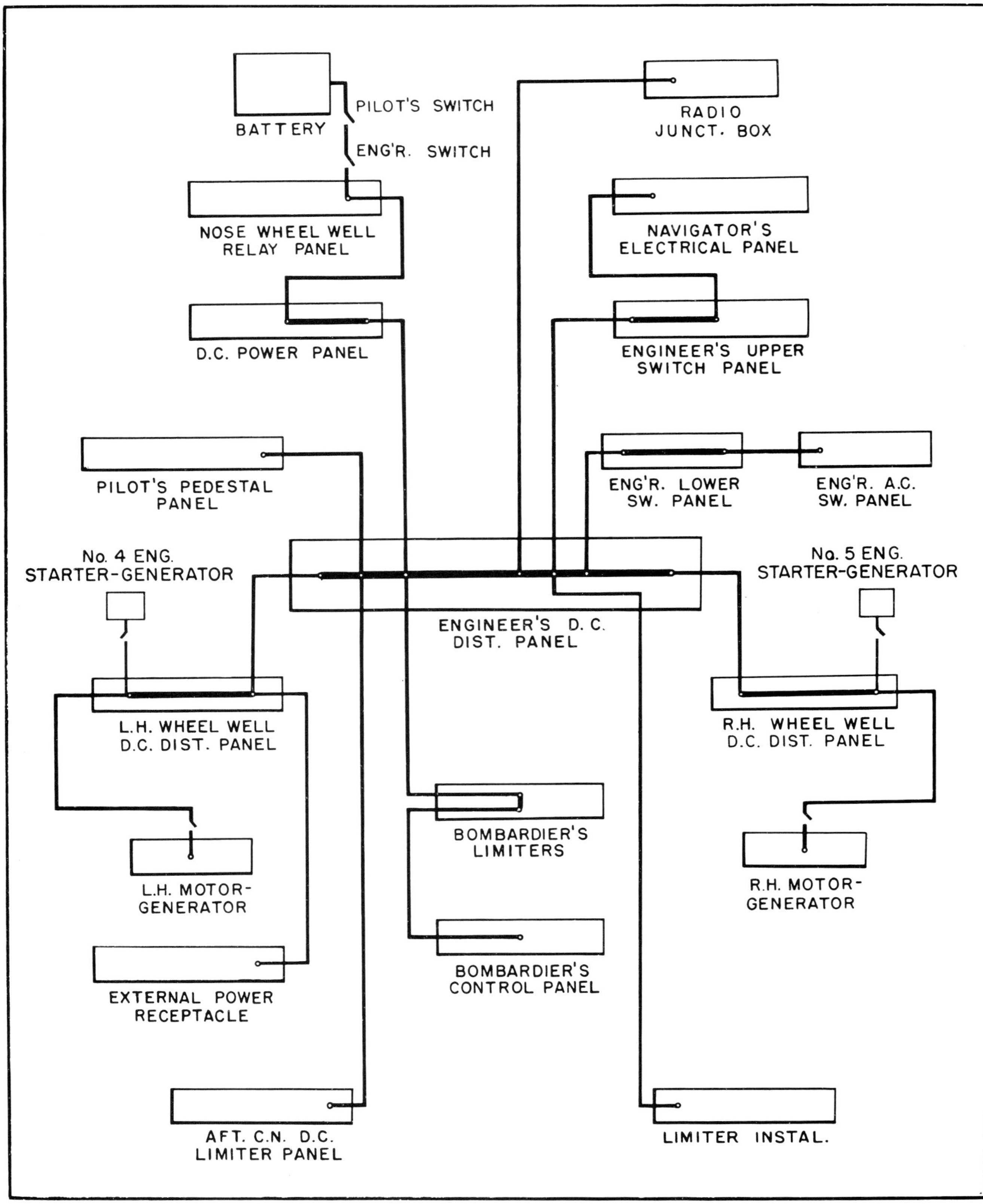

Figure 1-7. DC Power System

Figure 1-8. DC Control Panel

operate the inboard rudder and elevon actuators. The systems are entirely automatic and have been designed so that if three pumps on each side of the airplane should fail, there would be sufficient hydraulic power to operate the flight surfaces.

1-65. HYDRAULIC POWER BOOST SYSTEMS GAGES. (See 19 figure 1-12.)- A pressure gage for each system is located on a panel below the engineer's instrument panel.

1-66. HYDRAULIC BRAKE AND NOSE WHEEL STEERING SYSTEM.

1-67. GENERAL.- Two ac motor-driven pumps supply 3000 psi hydraulic pressure for the operation of the main gear brakes and the nose gear steering unit. (See figure 1-13.)

This system operates only when the landing gear is extended and the main gear forward fairing doors are closed. However, the main pump can be started at any time by means of an override switch at the engineer's station.

1-68. MANUAL OVERRIDE SWITCH. (See 16 figure 1-12.)- This two-position switch is protected by a red guard and is identified as HYD. BRAKE PUMP MANUAL OVERRIDE. It may be used in flight to check the operation of the hydraulic system or in an emergency when the system will not operate because of emergency lowering of the landing gear, failure of the normal operating switches, or control circuit.

1-69. BRAKE AND NOSE WHEEL STEERING SYSTEM PRESSURE GAGE. (See 15 figure 1-12.)- A single gage located below the engineer's instrument panel is used to register the pressure in this system.

1-70. ACCUMULATOR PRESSURE GAGE. (See 23 figure 1-2.)- An accumulator pressure gage for the brakes and nose wheel steering system is located just forward of the pilots' instrument panel. The gage can be read from the copilot's or bombardier's station and should register 600 psi air pressure.

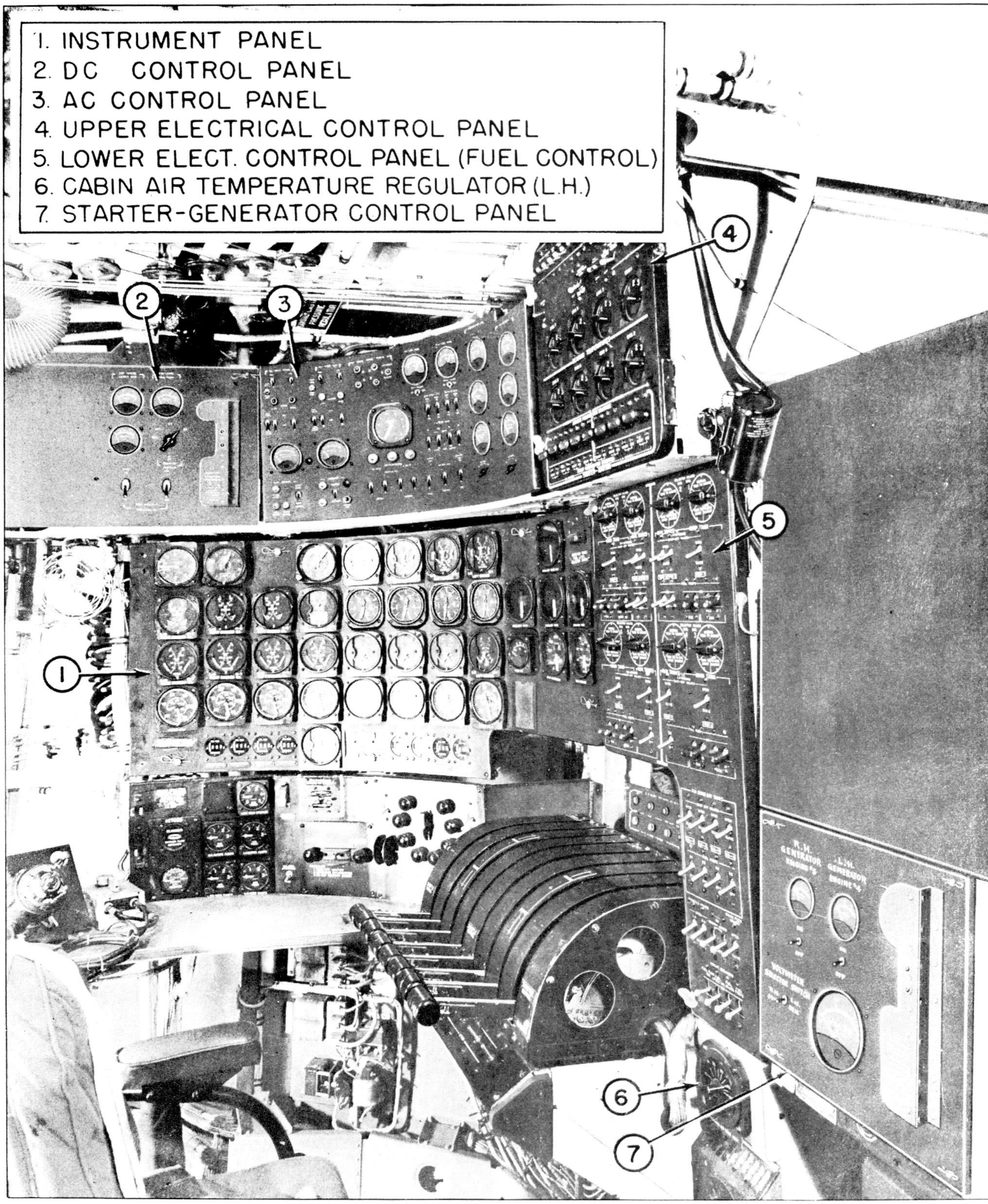

Figure 1-9. Engineer's Station

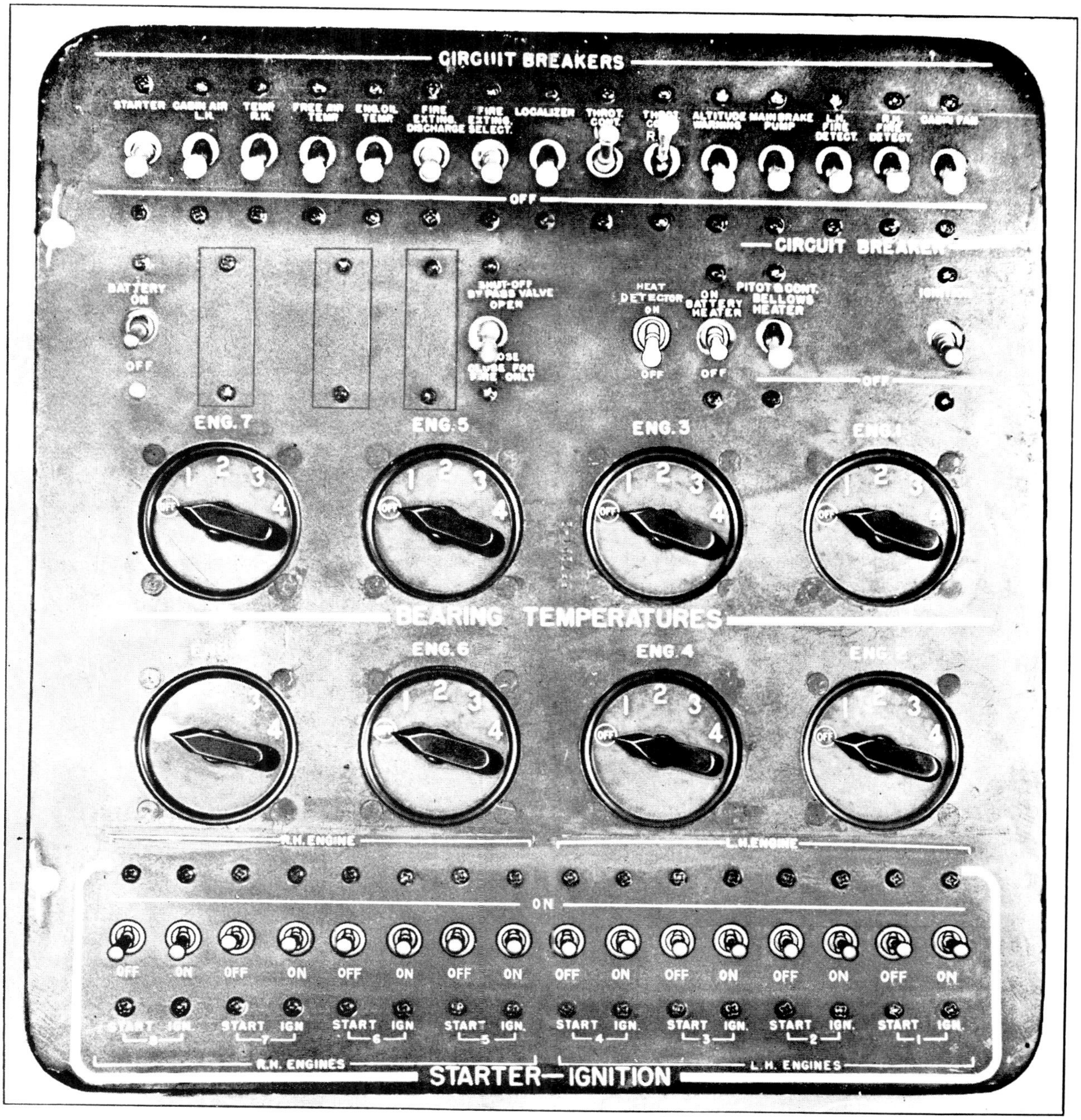

Figure 1-10. Engineer's Upper Electrical Control Panel

1-71. ENGINES.

1-72. GENERAL. (See figure 1-14.)

1-73. The airplane is powered by eight J-35-A-5 turbo-jet engines which produce a total thrust of 32,000 pounds. The engines in the left wing are numbered from 1 through 4 and in the right wing 5 through 8.

1-74. STARTING AND IGNITION SYSTEMS.

1-75. GENERAL.- Each engine is equipped with a direct cranking 28v dc starter. The starters on Nos. 4 and 5 engines are utilized as generators. The ignition operate on 120v ac.

1-76. STARTER AND IGNITION SWITCHES. (See figure 1-10.)- A starter and ignition switch is furnished for each engine. The starter

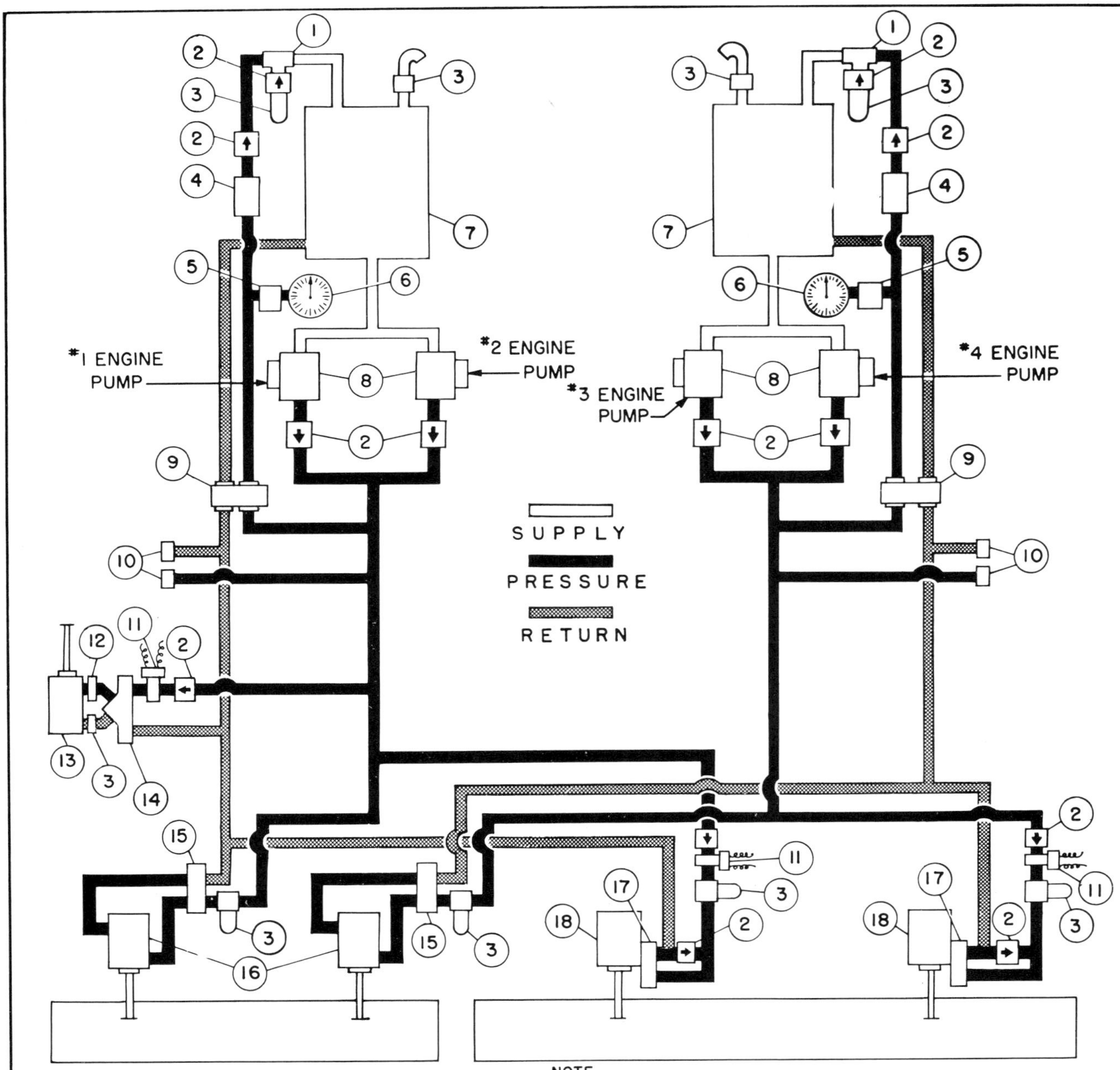

1. ASPIRATOR
2. CHECK VALVE
3. FILTER
4. RESTRICTOR & FILTER
5. GAGE LINE FUSE
6. PRESSURE GAGE
7. RESERVOIR
8. PUMPS, VARIABLE VOLUME
9. RELIEF VALVE
10. GROUND TEST CONNECTIONS
11. SOLENOID VALVE
12. RESTRICTOR
13. SLOT DOOR CYLINDER
14. VALVE
15. RUDDER SERVO VALVE
16. RUDDER CYLINDER
17. ELEVON SERVO VALVE
18. ELEVON CYLINDER

Figure 1-11. Hydraulic Power Boost System

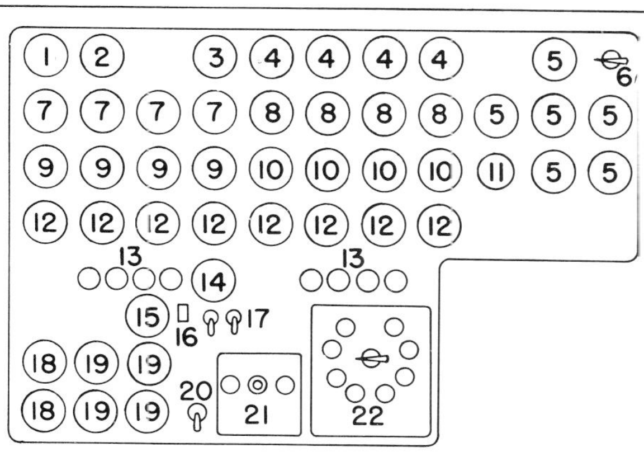

1. CABIN RATE OF CLIMB
2. CABIN ALTIMETER
3. ALTIMETER
4. BEARING TEMPERATURE INDICATORS
5. FUEL LEVEL INDICATORS
6. BOMB BAY TANKS FUEL LEVEL SELECTOR SWITCH
7. OIL TEMPERATURE INDICATORS
8. FUEL PRESSURE INDICATORS
9. OIL PRESSURE INDICATORS
10. TAIL PIPE TEMPERATURE INDICATORS
11. CABIN TEMPERATURE INDICATOR
12. ENGINE TACHOMETERS
13. FUEL COUNTER INDICATORS
14. APU CYLINDER HEAD TEMPERATURE INDICATORS
15. BRAKES AND NOSE WHEEL STEERING HYDRAULIC PRESSURE INDICATOR
16. BRAKES AND NOSE WHEEL STEERING HYDRAULIC PUMP OVERRIDE SWITCH
17. APU COOLING AIR VALVE CONTROL SWITCHES
18. OXYGEN INSTRUMENTS
19. HYDRAULIC POWER BOOST SYSTEM PRESSURE INDICATORS
20. GROUND CREW INTERPHONE SWITCH
21. APU FIRE EXTINGUISHER CONTROLS
22. ENGINE FIRE EXTINGUISHER CONTROLS

Figure 1-12. Engineer's Instrument Panel

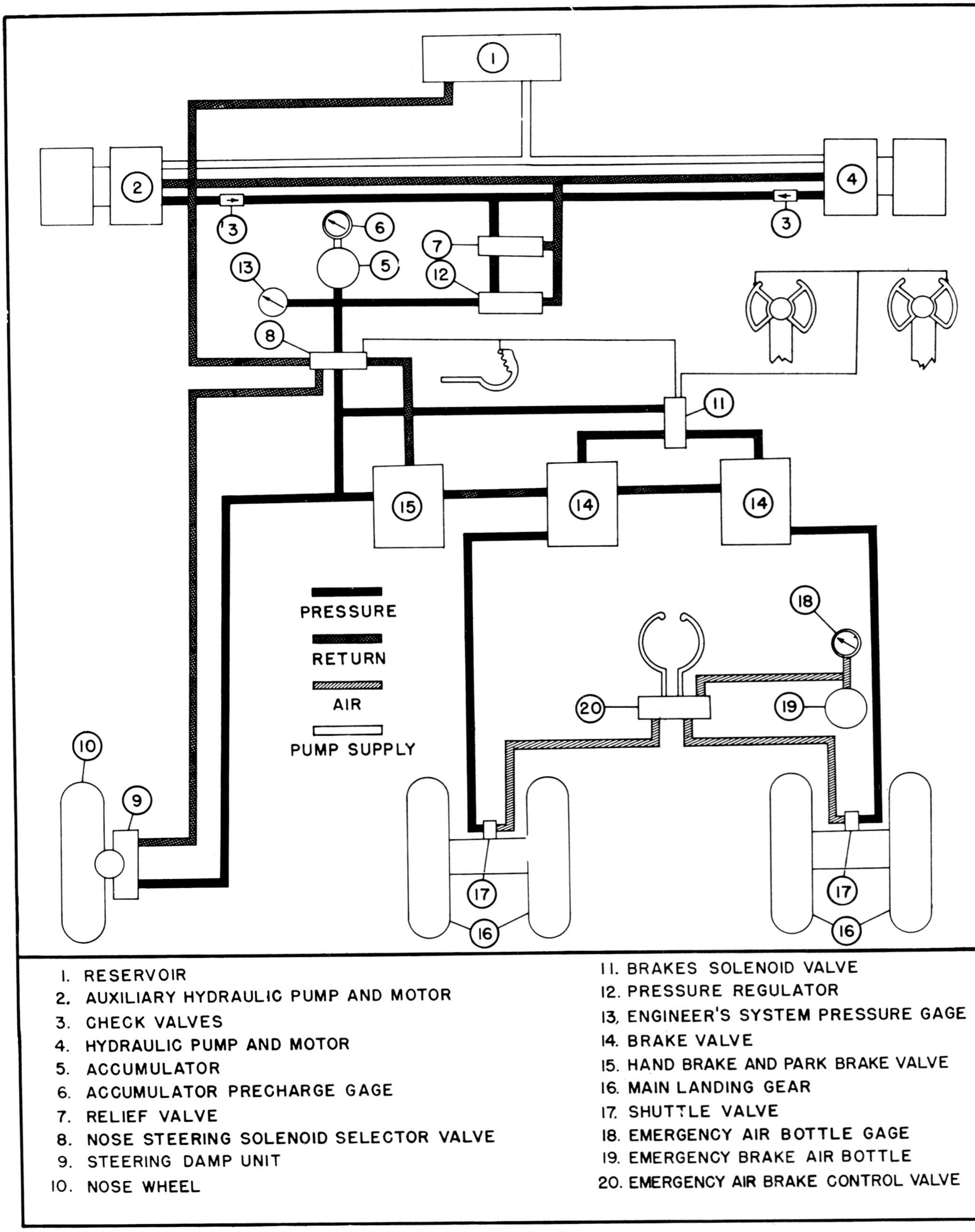

1. RESERVOIR
2. AUXILIARY HYDRAULIC PUMP AND MOTOR
3. CHECK VALVES
4. HYDRAULIC PUMP AND MOTOR
5. ACCUMULATOR
6. ACCUMULATOR PRECHARGE GAGE
7. RELIEF VALVE
8. NOSE STEERING SOLENOID SELECTOR VALVE
9. STEERING DAMP UNIT
10. NOSE WHEEL
11. BRAKES SOLENOID VALVE
12. PRESSURE REGULATOR
13. ENGINEER'S SYSTEM PRESSURE GAGE
14. BRAKE VALVE
15. HAND BRAKE AND PARK BRAKE VALVE
16. MAIN LANDING GEAR
17. SHUTTLE VALVE
18. EMERGENCY AIR BOTTLE GAGE
19. EMERGENCY BRAKE AIR BOTTLE
20. EMERGENCY AIR BRAKE CONTROL VALVE

Figure 1-13. Brakes and Nose Wheel Steering Hydraulic System

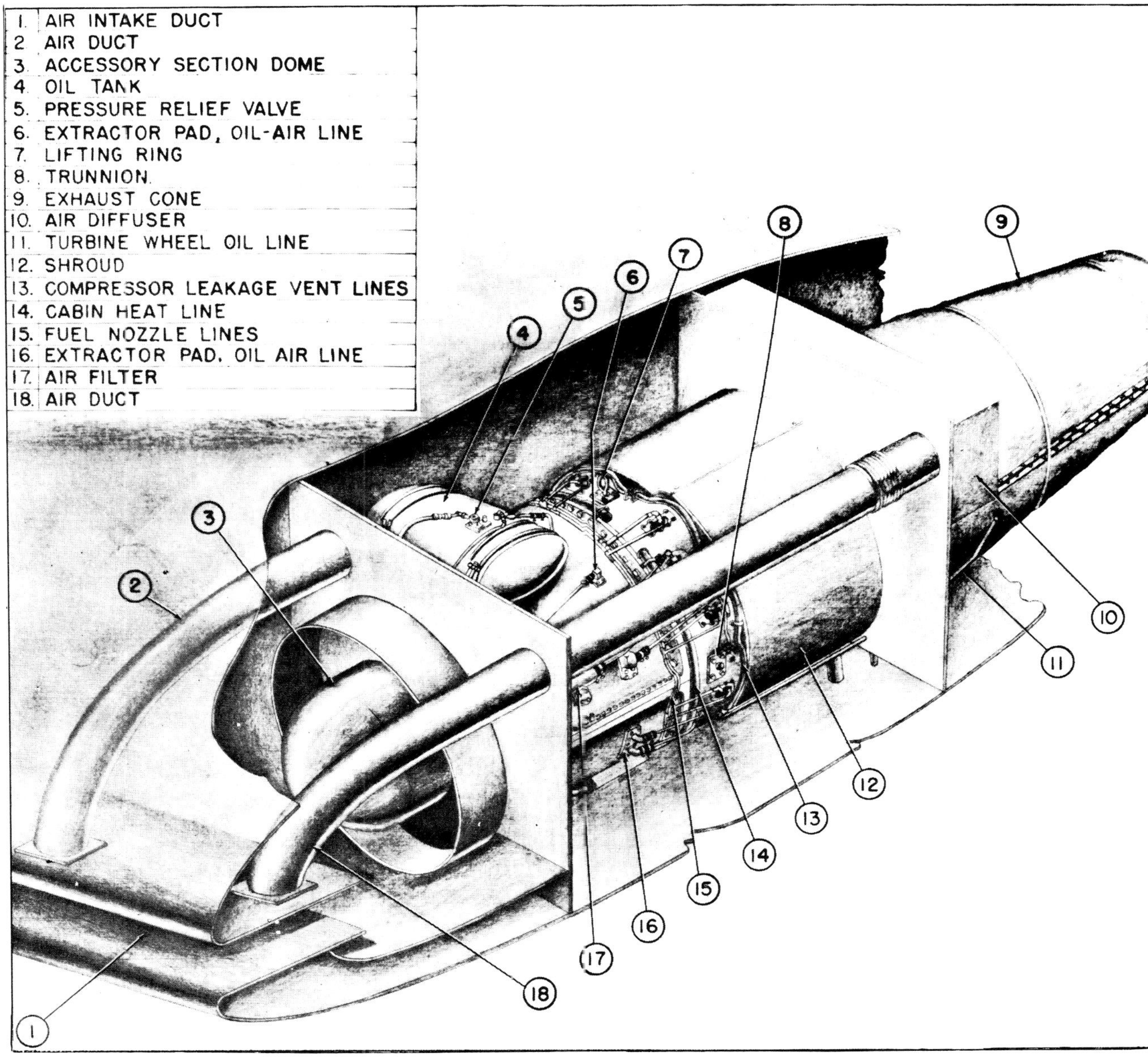

Figure 1-14. Engine Compartment Arrangement

switches have two positions and the ignition switches are spring-loaded to the "OFF" position. The ignition switches are used for starting only.

1-77. AIR INTAKE SYSTEM. (See figure 1-15.)

1-78. INDUCTION AIR.- Induction air to the engine compressors is admitted through the leading edge of the wing where it is led directly to each engine through its respective main duct. There are no controls for induction air.

1-79. ENGINE COMPARTMENT COOLING AIR.- Inasmuch as very little cooling air is required for the engines, the prime purpose of admitting cooling air into the engine compartments is for structure cooling. In this airplane a reversing flow system is used to provide adequate cooling air for ground operations. Each engine compartment is divided into a forward and tail pipe section. Two ducts having their take-offs in the main engine induction duct supply these compartments. Cooling air for the forward compartment is normally expelled through louvers in the engine bay doors and the tail pipe cooling air is emitted through a shroud around the tail pipe. When the engines are operating on the ground, a low pressure area at the intake ducts reverses the flow of cooling air so that air is taken in at the louvers and tail pipe and expelled into the main duct. In flight, ram air dispells the low pressure areas and flows through the engine compartments to be emitted through the louvers

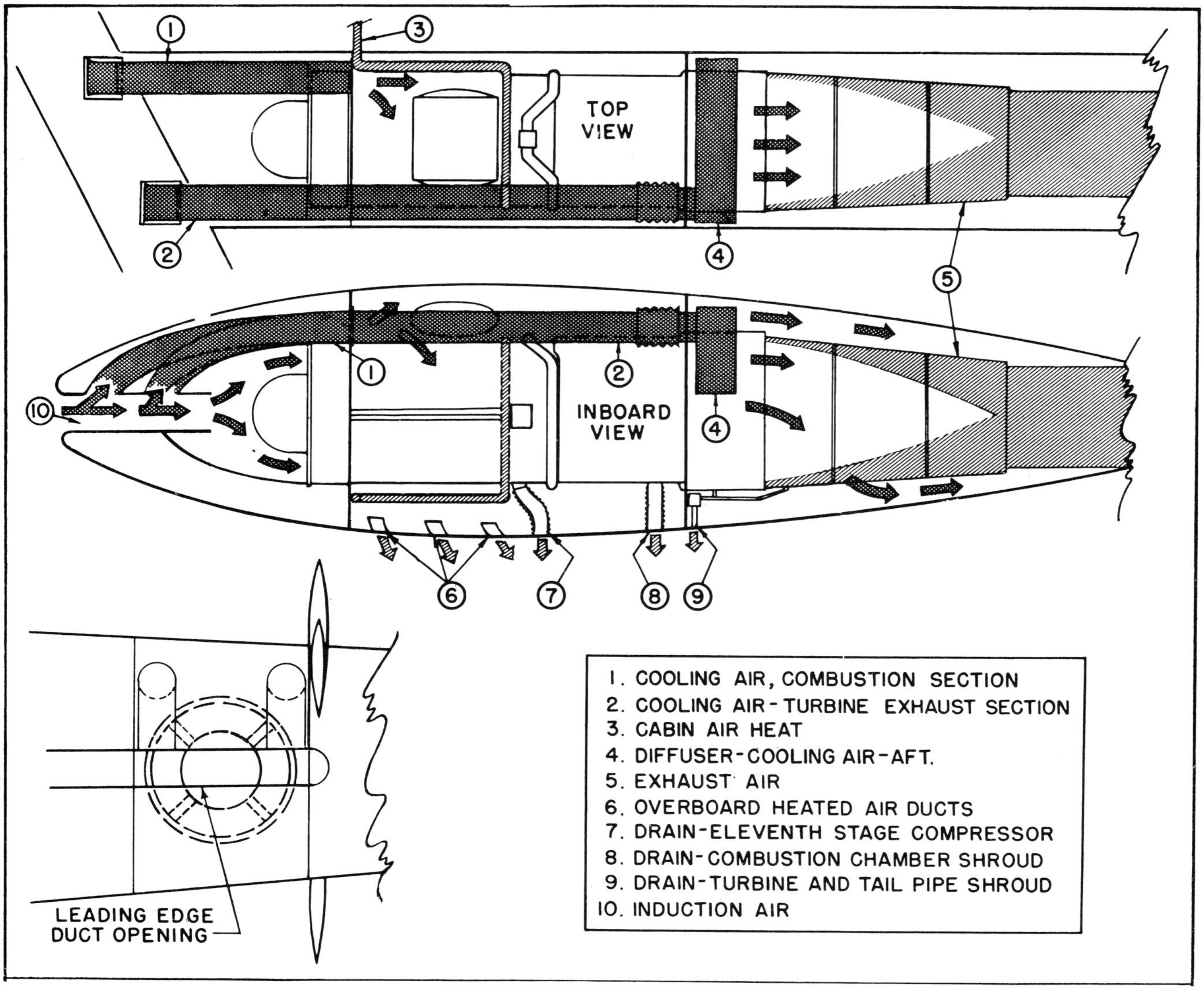

Figure 1-15. Engine Compartment Airflow - Schematic

and tail pipe shroud. This type of system has a characteristic that at a certain airspeed in relation to engine power setting there will be a transition where the ram air will equal the low pressure area and consequently create a lag in the flow of cooling air. This transition will generally occur shortly after take-off where full power is used and as the climb speed is set.

1-80. ENGINE TEMPERATURE INDICATORS.

1-81. BEARING TEMPERATURE GAGES AND SELECTOR SWITCHES. (See figure 1-10 and 4 figure 1-12.)- Four dual-indicating gages are provided to register bearing temperatures, and eight four-position selector switches (one for each engine) are used to select the particular bearing for which a temperature reading is desired. Each selector switch has positions numbered 1 through 4, indicating the four engine bearings. By moving a selector switch from one bearing position to another, individual bearing temperatures will register on the respective indicator gage. There are no controls for regulating bearing temperatures.

1-82. TAIL PIPE TEMPERATURE INDICATORS. (See 10, figure 1-12.)- Four dual-indicating temperature gages are installed on the engineer's instrument panel for registering tail pipe temperatures. There are no direct controls for regulating tail pipe temperatures, however tail pipe temperatures can be indirectly controlled by throttle settings.

1-83. FUEL REGULATOR CONTROLS.

1-84. GENERAL.- Each engine is equipped with a fuel regulator which controls the fuel pressure supplied to the combustion chambers of the engine. The regulators are operated

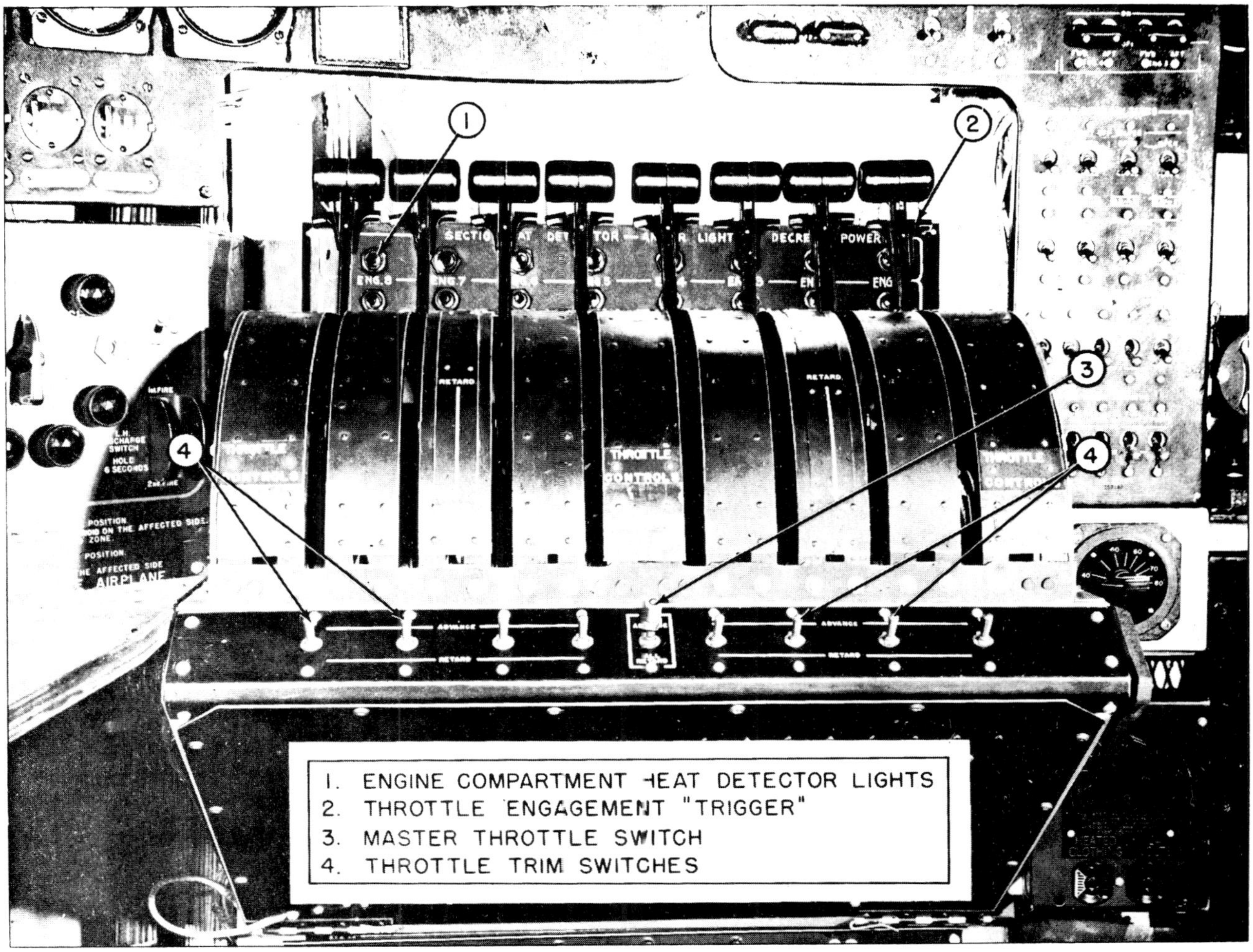

Figure 1-16. Engineer's Throttle Quadrant

by throttle controls at the pilots' or engineer's stations. (See figures 1-16 and 1-23.) The throttles can be operated manually or electrically. Manual control is used for take-off, landing and in the event of electrical failure. The engineer is provided with one throttle lever for each engine and the pilots with one lever for each bank of four engines. Each of the engineer's throttle levers is permanently connected to its respective fuel regulator by a cable system. (See figure 1-17 for identification of items.) A pilots' follow-up arm assembly and a motor-drive bellcrank are installed beside each lever in the engineer's throttle unit. The bellcrank is linked to a dc motor-drive and the arm assembly is cable-connected to one of the pilots' throttle levers. Two triggers, operating together beneath each throttle handle, move a pin on each throttle lever which engages a notch in the bellcrank and arm assembly. The triggers have three positions. (See figure 1-18.) First when raised up all the way, the pins clear both the bellcranks and the arm assemblies allowing the engineer to move any throttle independently of the others in its bank, the pilots' levers, and the dc motor drives. Second, each of the engineer's levers is recessed on one side for about half of the downward trigger travel. When the lower end of one trigger is engaged in the recess, the pin can only be engaged with the arm assembly. The trigger will engage the recess when the EMERGENCY DISENGAGE levers are moved to manual. This affords manual control of the throttles in banks of four for the pilots and engineer. Third, lifting the one trigger that is engaged in the recess and pressing down on the other permits the engineer to engage the pins with the bellcranks. (See figure 1-18.) This allows the throttles to be controlled electrically by movement of the pilots' levers, the engineer's MASTER THROTTLE switch or individual TRIM switches. The pilots' EMERGENCY DISENGAGE levers must be in the automatic position (up) in order for the engineer to engage his levers with the motor-drives. When the EMERGENCY DISENGAGE levers are in the manual (down) position (see figure 1-24) a sliding plate blocks the notch in the motor-drive bellcrank, disengaging the motor-drives from the throttles.

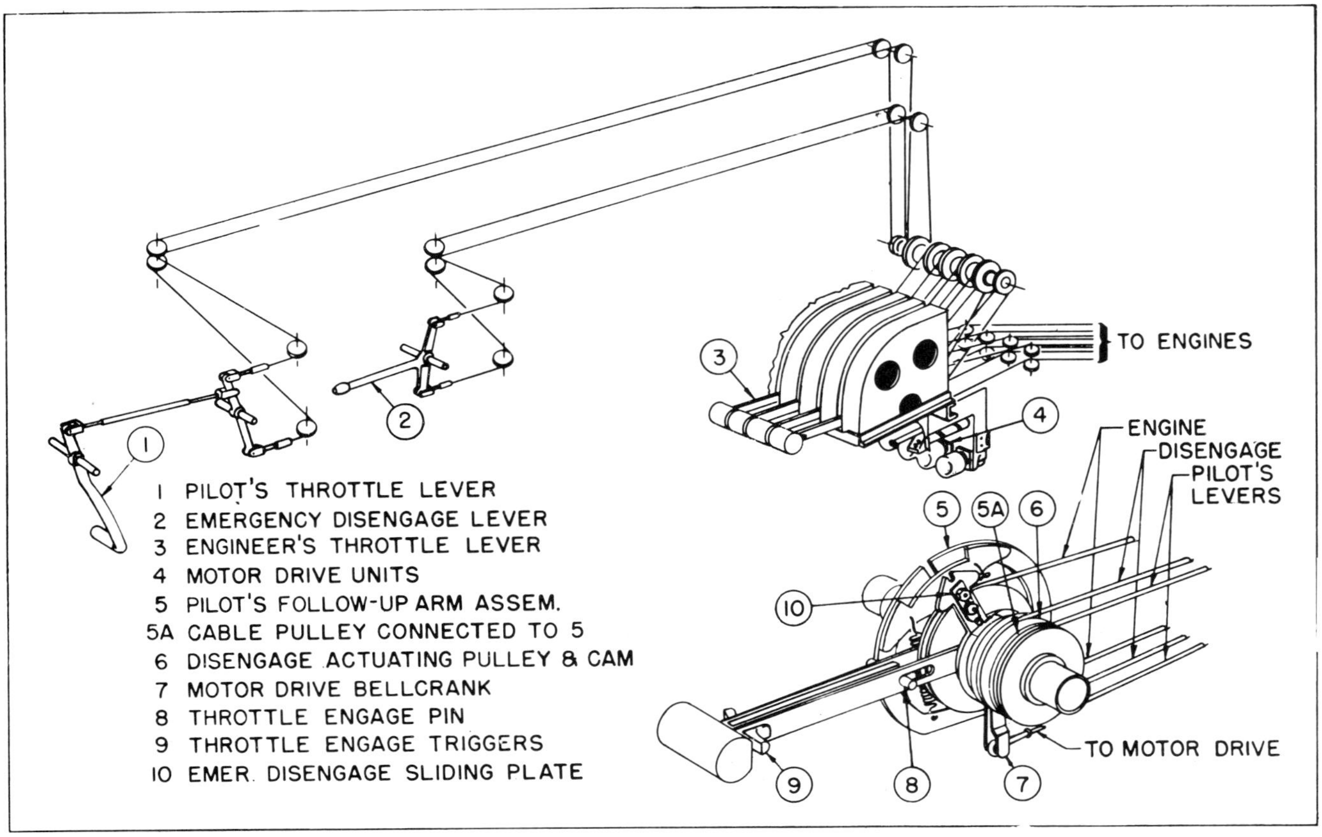

Figure 1-17. Throttle System

A push-button switch on each of the pilots' throttle levers permits high-speed electric operation of the throttles. Use of these push-buttons will operate the electric drive at three times the normal speed and is intended for use at altitudes below 10,000 feet. The normal electric control will operate the throttles at safe speeds regardless of altitude. When using manual control, particularly above 10,000 feet, the throttles can easily be moved too fast. A too fast advance of the throttles results in high tail pipe temperatures which may burn up the turbine wheels, and a too fast retard can blow out the fires in the combustion chambers. Therefore the following usage of the throttles should be observed; move the throttles very slowly observing tail pipe temperatures for limits when on manual control. Use the high speed button only below 10,000 feet when on electric control. To best describe the operation of the throttle system it is divided into two sections, manual and electric throttle control.

1-85. MANUAL THROTTLE CONTROL.- Manual control of the throttles can be accomplished in two different manners as follows: First, individual manual throttle control may be effected by the engineer by raising the triggers on the throttle lever (which disengages the pin in the motor-drive bellcrank and arm assembly) and moving the lever throughout the full range of travel. (See figure 1-19.) This procedure is used for starting and stopping individual engines. If the engineer stops an engine while in flight this method will disengage and close that one throttle. (See figure 1-19.) This will not affect the operation of the other throttles whether on manual or electric control. Second, manual control of all throttles is possible by moving the pilots' EMERGENCY DISENGAGE levers to the manual (down) position. (See figure 1-24.) When this is done the notches in the motor-drive bellcranks will be blocked, disconnecting the electric control. As long as the engineer leaves his throttle levers engaged with the pilots' quadrants, both engineer and pilots will have manual control of the throttles and either can retard the throttles to 35% rpm. (See figure 1-20.) Movement of at least two throttles in each bank of four at the engineer's throttle unit will move all throttles, and movement of the pilots' levers will also move all throttles. The engineer cannot reengage the motor-drives until the pilot places the EMERGENCY DISENGAGE levers in the automatic position (up). This type of manual control is used for take-off and landing so that the throttles will be independent of the motor-drives and can be cut more quickly and also for use in the event that the dc motor-drives should malfunction.

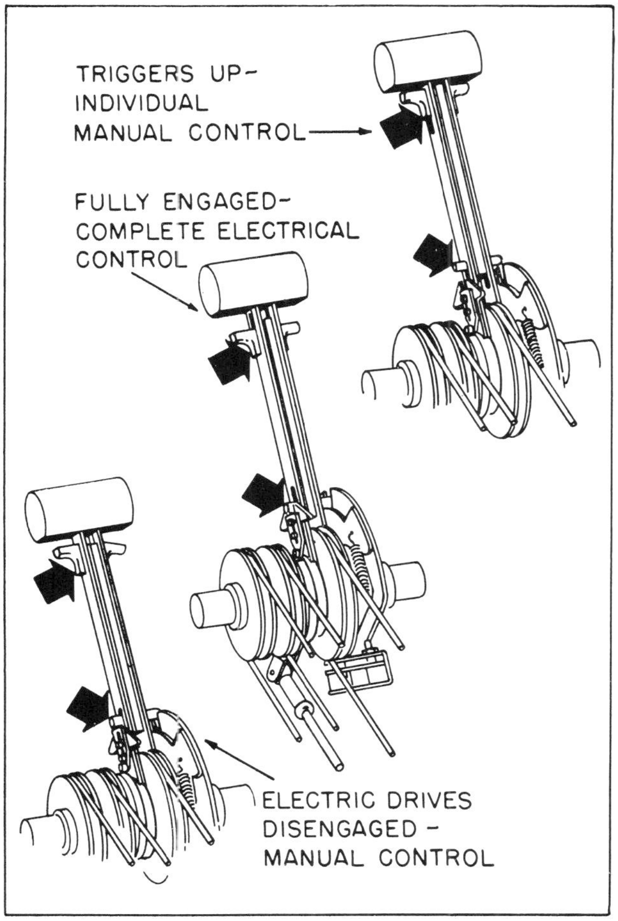

Figure 1-18. Throttle Lever Engagement Triggers

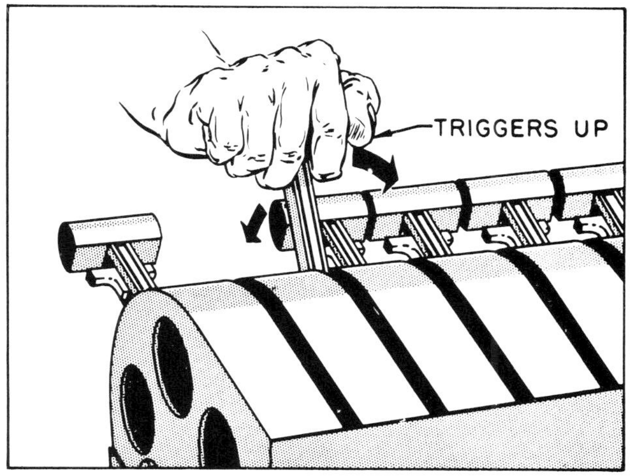

Figure 1-19. Individual Manual Throttle Control - Engineer

When using manual control be sure to move the throttles very slowly (approximately 30 seconds from 27% rpm to full advanced) to avoid overheating of the tail pipes or blowing out the fires.

1-86. ELECTRIC THROTTLE CONTROL.- The engineer cannot engage the throttle levers with the motor-drive bellcranks until they are first engaged with the pilots' follow-up arm assemblies. Likewise he cannot engage the motor-drives unless the pilots' EMERGENCY DISENGAGE levers are in the automatic position. To engage the electric system the engineer must first operate the motor-drives so that the bellcranks can be located for engagement with the throttle levers. On the ground this can be accomplished by holding the MASTER switch to the "ADVANCE" posi-

Figure 1-20. Manual Throttle Control - Pilots and Engineer

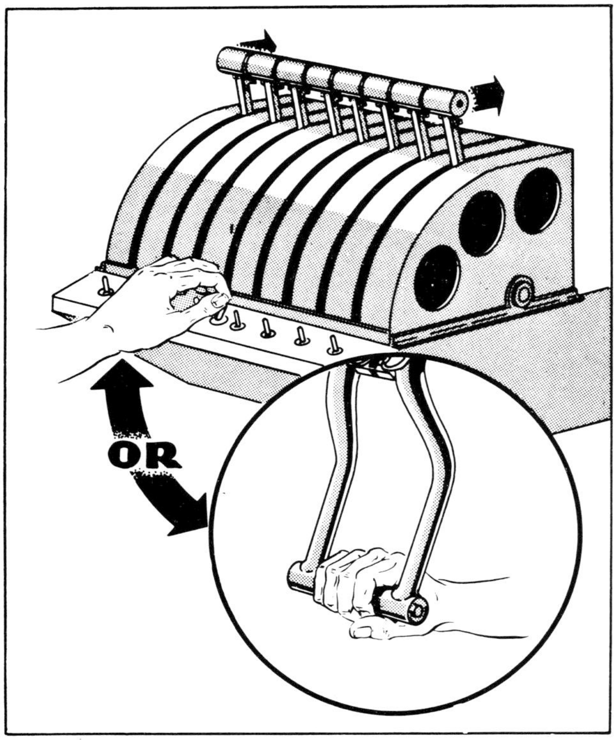

Figure 1-21. Electric Throttle Control - Pilots and Engineer

tion until the motor-drives stop and then to the "RETARD" position until the motors stop again. By doing this the engineer will know that all bellcranks are in line at the 65% rpm position. In flight the motor-drives can be left at the advanced position to save retarding the throttles to a low rpm for engagement. In either case engagement is the same; lift the one trigger to clear the recess in the lever and press down on the other while holding the respective TRIM switch to "RETARD." When the motor-drive bellcrank reaches the same position as the lever, the pin will engage in the bellcrank notch and

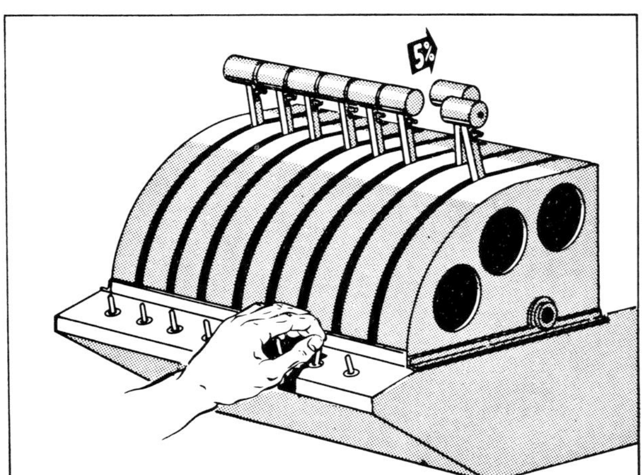

Figure 1-22. Throttle Trim Operation - Engineer

the triggers will move full down. After all throttles have been engaged in this manner, the pilots and engineer will have complete control. (See figure 1-21.) Using a follow-up movement of both levers the pilots have a range of control from 65% rpm to full advanced. 65% rpm is a minimum for altitudes above 10,000 feet. Below 10,000 feet the pilots can retard the throttles to 50% rpm by holding one of the HIGH SPEED push buttons while moving the throttles back. The engineer's MASTER switch provides a range of control between 65% rpm and full advanced, moving all eight throttles simultaneously. If the levers are below 65% rpm and engaged with the motor-drives, as in the case when the trim switches are used to retard the drives for throttle engagement below 65% rpm, the master switch can be used to advance all throttles. The individual TRIM switches allow a throttle to be advanced or retarded a minimum of 5% rpm in relation to the position of the other throttles for the purpose of synchronizing engine rpms without disengaging a throttle and operating it manually. (See figure 1-22.) The trim switches will move the throttles from 65% rpm to below minimum idle position.

1-87. FUEL SYSTEM.

1-88. GENERAL.

1-89. The system consists of four main tanks which feed the eight engines either directly or through an engine manifold line. In addition there are six auxiliary and four bomb bay tanks which feed the main tanks through an auxiliary-tank-manifold line and individual main tank supply lines. Controls are also provided so that auxiliary and bomb bay fuel can by-pass the main tanks and feed directly into the engine-manifold-line. Fuel transfer from one main tank to another is possible through the manifold lines and the main tank supply lines. Overflow of the main tanks is prevented by fuel level valves which automatically close the main tank supply lines when these tanks are full. Each main tank is equipped with four ac-driven, single speed, fuel booster pumps; each pump has a capacity exceeding the maximum requirements of one engine. One booster pump is installed in each auxiliary and bomb bay tank. All pumps are equipped with check valves to prevent reverse flow through a pump into an empty tank. All fuel controls are located on the engineer's lower electrical control panel. (See figure 1-26.) JP-1 fuel, Specification AN-F-32 is used in this airplane. Due to the installation of the A.P.U.'s in bomb bays 3 and 6, bomb bay tanks cannot be carried in these bays. Tank Capacities are as follows:

Main Tanks	1 and 4	1239 Gal. Ea.
Main Tank	2	1201 Gal.
Main Tank	3	1321 Gal.
B.B. Tanks	2 and 7	895 Gal. Ea.
Aux. Tanks	5 and 10	1573 Gal. Ea.
Aux. Tanks	6 and 9	887 Gal. Ea.
Aux. Tanks	7 and 8	1416 Gal. Ea.

(Total airplane fuel 14,542 Gal.)

1-90. FUEL CONTROLS.

1-91. ENGINE FUEL SELECTOR VALVE SWITCHES. (See figure 1-26.)- Fuel selection for each engine is made through a rotary-type, five position switch. These switches control the

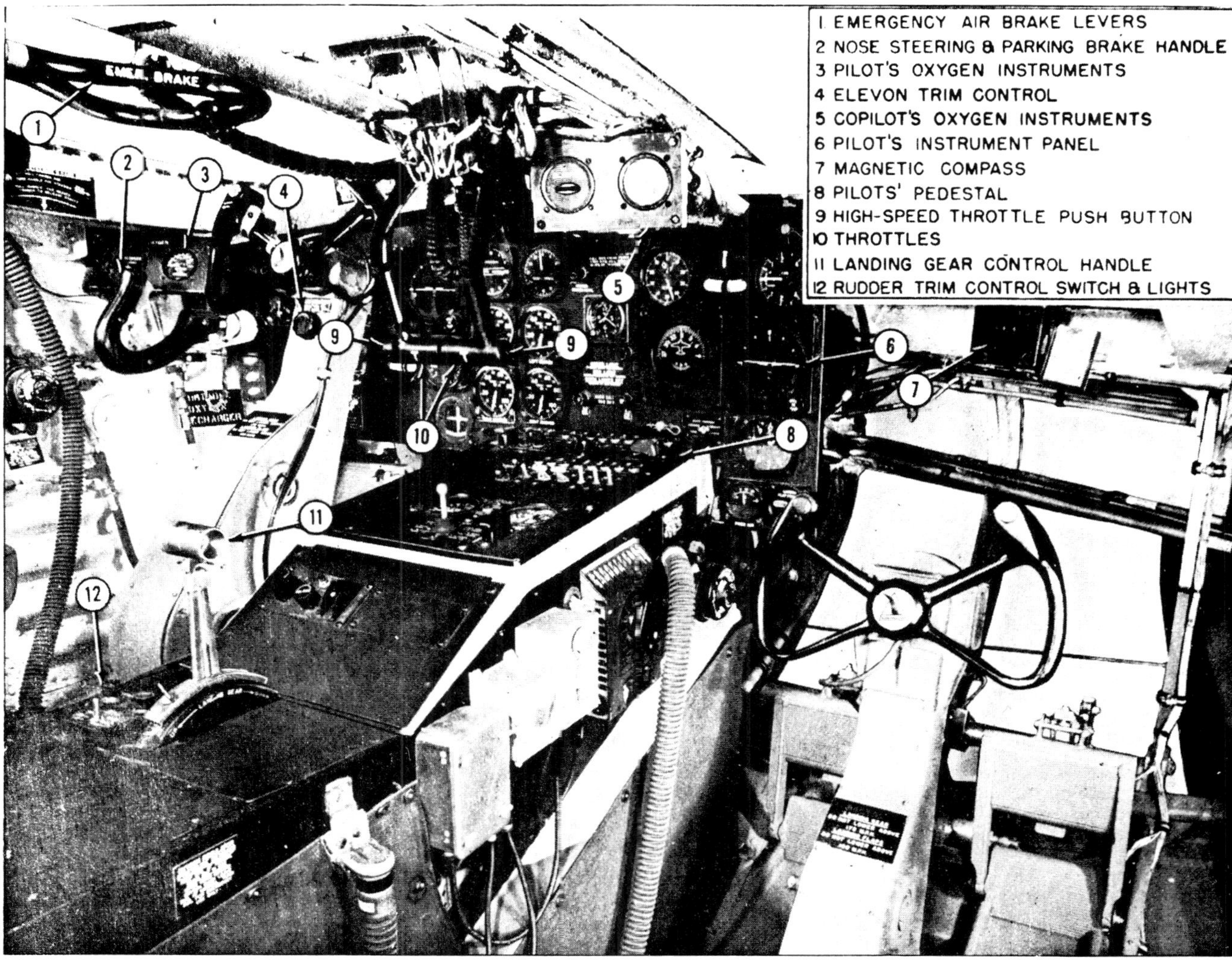

Figure 1-23. Pilot's Station

dc motor-operated selector valves so that any desired combination of fuel selection may be made.

1-92. MAIN TANK SUPPLY SHUT-OFF VALVE SWITCHES. (See figure 1-26.)- These four switches are used to shut off the main tank supply lines.

1-93. AUXILIARY AND BOMB BAY FUEL TANK SHUT-OFF VALVE SWITCHES. (See figure 1-26.)- Each auxiliary and bomb bay fuel tank is provided with an electrically controlled shut-off valve so that it may be shut off when it is emptied of fuel.

1-94. FUEL PUMP SWITCHES. (See figure 1-26.)- The four booster pumps in each main tank are connected in pairs. One forward and one aft constitute a pair. Eight pairs of switches are located on the engineer's lower electrical control panel with "ON-OFF" position for control of the pumps. Single switches are provided for control of the auxiliary tank pumps. Normally the main tank pumps are to be kept "ON" for all operations and the auxiliary pumps "ON" as long as fuel is being pumped from these tanks. When the auxiliary tanks are empty, the pumps should be turned "OFF."

1-95. MANIFOLD VALVE SWITCHES. (See figure 1-26.)- AC-operated manifold valves permit the flow of fuel between the auxiliary and engine-manifold lines. During normal operation the MANIFOLD VALVE switches are "CLOSED" allowing fuel from the auxiliary and bomb bay tanks to flow into the main fuel tanks. When "OPEN," fuel will flow into the engine-manifold-line where it can be distributed to the engines through the engine fuel selector valves instead of being pumped into the main fuel tanks.

1-96. CROSS-FEED VALVE SWITCHES. (See figure 1-26.)- Two ac motor-operated valves are installed in the manifold line to control the flow of fuel from one side of the airplane to the other. Two valves are used so that there will not be a "live" fuel line through the crew nacelle. A single switch is used to open or close the valves.

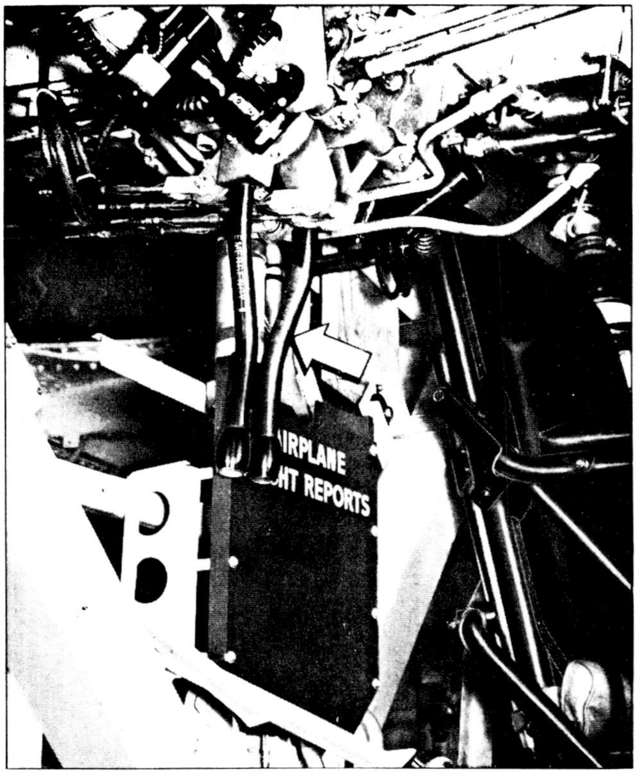

Figure 1-24. Emergency Throttle Disengage Levers

1-97. FUEL QUANTITY GAGES. (See 5 figure 1-12.)- Dual type indicators are used to register the fuel quantities in the main and auxiliary fuel tanks. A single indicator is provided for the auxiliary bomb bay tanks and a selector switch is used to select the bomb bay tank for which a reading is desired. The hands of the dual indicators are marked to identify the tanks.

1-98. FUEL COUNTER INDICATORS. (See 13 figure 1-12.)- One indicator is provided for each engine. These indicators can each be set to 999 gallons which does not total the entire fuel capacity of the airplane. For this reason the following is suggested for use of the indicators: if the airplane is carrying a total of 15,000 gallons of fuel, that total should be divided by eight which gives 1,875. This cannot be set on the indicators, but if the indicators are set to 875 they will subtract to zero and then start over again. In this manner, adding the amounts shown on the indicators will give the total fuel remaining in the airplane.

1-99. OIL SYSTEM.

1-100. GENERAL.

1-101. Lubrication is provided for the bearings of each engine from a self-contained oil system. A ten-gallon oil tank is attached to the top of the engine accessory section. Specification AN-O-8, Grade 1065 oil is used in this airplane. There are no controls for the oil systems.

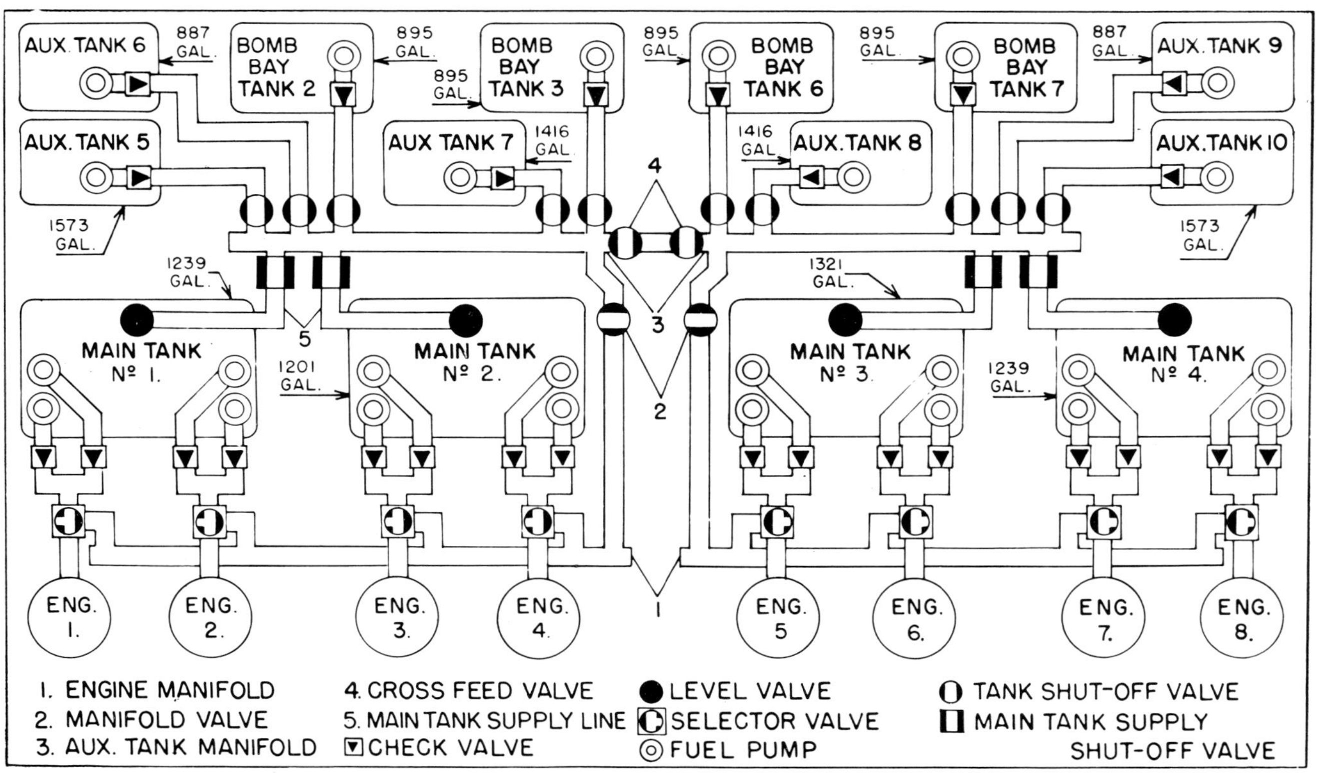

Figure 1-25. Fuel System - Schematic

Figure 1-26. Engineer's Lower Electrical Control Panel

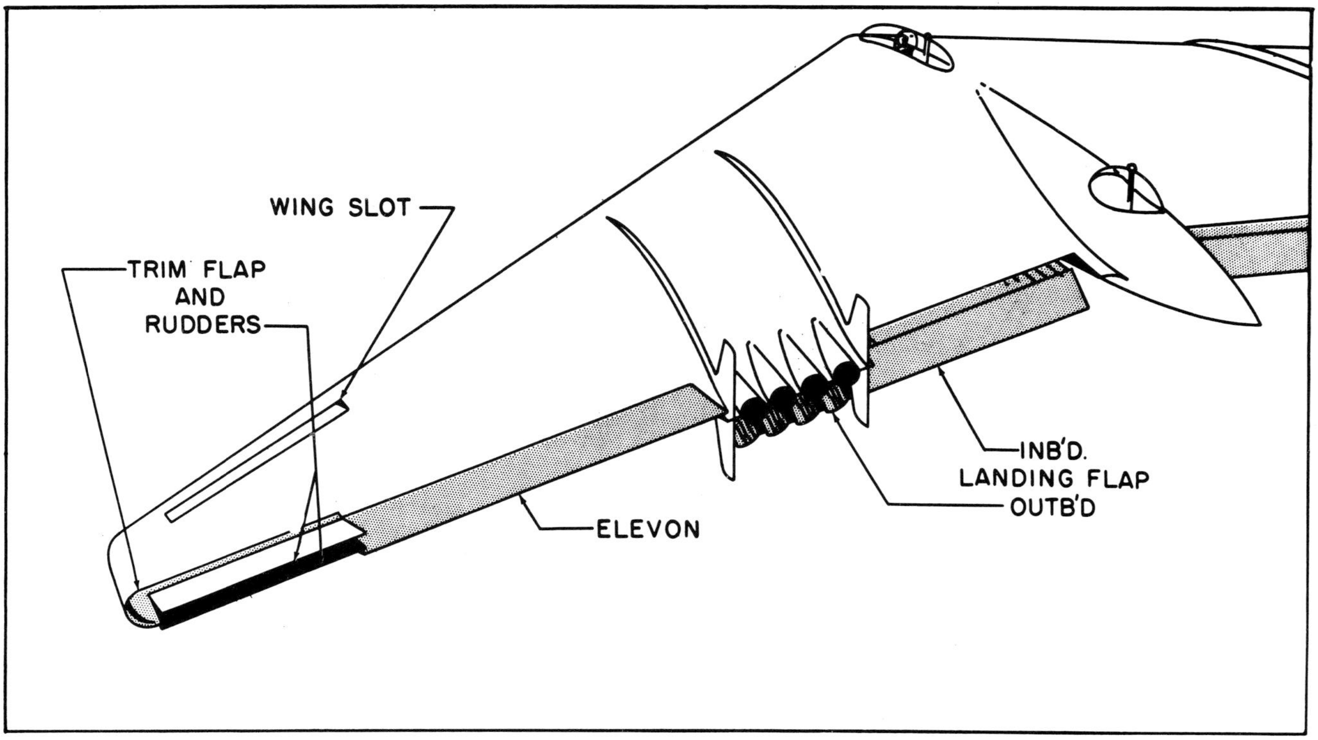

Figure 1-27. Flight Control Surfaces

1-102. OIL INDICATORS. (See 7 and 9 figure 1-12.)- There are four dual oil pressure indicators and four dual oil temperature indicators on the engineer's instrument panel.

1-103. FLIGHT SURFACE CONTROLS.

1-104. GENERAL. (See figure 1-27.)

1-105. The flight surfaces control this airplane in a normal manner, although their action is somewhat unconventional. Instead of using ailerons and elevators, this airplane is equipped with elevons which provide lateral and longitudinal control. These surfaces are actuated by hydraulic pressure, but are controlled by conventional control columns and wheels. The rudders are also actuated by hydraulic pressure and act as drag surfaces to create a turning moment rather than conventional deflection-type rudder. The rudder pedals are not interconnected as in most airplanes, but operate independently of each other. Each rudder is hinged to an electrically-operated trim flap. The trim flaps are used for pitch and roll trim. The rudders move with the trim flaps for trim purposes but operate independently for directional control. Hydraulically actuated wing slot doors are used to close the wing slots in the leading edge of each wing. The slots are provided to prevent wing tip stall at low speeds. Conventional landing flaps are electrically operated and controlled. Inasmuch as the elevons and rudders are power-operated, it has been necessary to provide an artificial "feel" to the controls for these surfaces. This has been accomplished by springs attached to the control wheel and rudder mechanisms which return the controls to neutral and also provide the "feel" necessary to prevent overcontrol of the rudders and "aileron" movement of the elevons. A control force bellows, utilizing ram air pressure over static air, provides "feel" to the operation of the control columns for "elevator" control. There are no control surface locks. The fluid in the hydraulic actuating cylinders provides a fluid lock which prevents the surfaces from moving when the airplane is not in use.

1-106. CONTROL FORCE BELLOWS.

1-107. GENERAL.- A control force bellows is attached to the pilot's control column to lend proportional "feel" only to the operation of the column for "elevator" control. (See figure 1-28.) It is a cylindrical assembly incorporating a bellows diaphragm. The method of attachment to the control column is such that movement of a column in either direction moves the diaphragm in the same direction, against the ram air pressure. When the airplane is resting on the ground, static air is in both sides of the bellows compartments, so there is no feel of the bellows on control column movement. In flight ram air creates a pressure on the aft side of the diaphragm which must be overcome to move a column. It is apparent then that pressure increases with speed, and consequently the higher the airspeed the more resistance to control column movement. To forestall icing

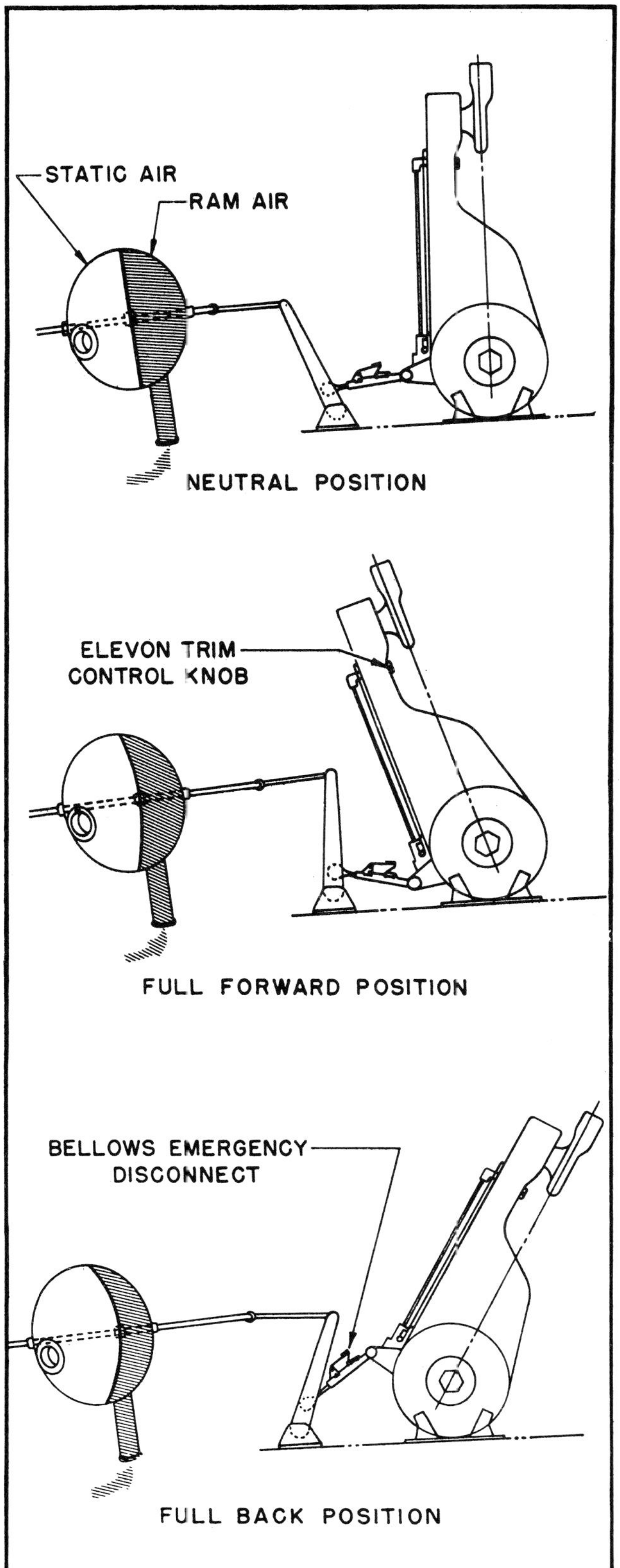

Figure 1-28. Control Force Bellows Action

dangers, an electric heating element installed in the bellows can be used at the pilot's discretion. The linkage connecting the bellows to the pilot's column can be disconnected by a disengage lever.

1-108. CONTROL FORCE BELLOWS HEATER SWITCH. (See figure 1-10.)- The control force bellows dc heater element is controlled by a two-position switch on the engineer's upper electrical control panel. This switch also controls the pitot tube heaters. It is identified as PITOT AND CONTR. BELLOWS HEATER.

1-109. CONTROL FORCE BELLOWS DISENGAGE LEVER. (See figure 1-28.)- The control bellows connecting linkage attaches to the forward side of the pilot's control column. At this point a lever is provided which can be raised to disconnect the linkage and free the column from the bellows.

NOTE

If disengaged, the bellows cannot be re-engaged while in flight.

1-110. ELEVONS.

1-111. GENERAL.- The elevons function as both elevators and ailerons. They are actuated by hydraulic cylinders which obtain operating pressure from the Hydraulic Power Boost Systems. Pressure to the hydraulic actuating cylinders is regulated by servo valves that are operated by the control columns and wheels, through cable systems. An emergency elevon system is provided whereby the elevons may be operated by electric motors in the event of a hydraulic power failure.

1-112. NORMAL ELEVON CONTROL.- Fore-and-aft movement of a control column moves both elevons together as elevators. Turning a control wheel moves the elevons in opposite directions, in a manner similar to conventional ailerons. Simultaneous movement of the columns and wheels results in a combined elevator and aileron action as illustrated in figure 1-29.

1-113. EMERGENCY ELEVON CONTROL.

1-114. GENERAL.- Emergency elevon control is provided by reversible dc motors. When the emergency system is engaged, the normal hydraulic power is by-passed and the motors are operated by follow-up switch-and-cam assemblies actuated by the normal cable system. The switches are operated by cams to open and close the motor circuits, starting and stopping the motors which drive the elevons. In the event of a dc power system failure, the airplane battery will automatically be cut into the control circuit. The starter-generators may be turned on for unlimited operation of this system.

1-115. EMERGENCY ELEVON SWITCHES. (See 2 figure 1-30 and figure 1-33.)- Two switches control the emergency system. One switch on the pilot's control wheel can be used to make a momentary check of the system and another switch on the pilots' pedestal is

Figure 1-29. Elevon and Rudder Action

used to engage the system. After engaging the system the control may be operated normally and there is sufficient power to completely control the airplane at airspeeds below 200 mph.

1-116. EMERGENCY ELEVON LOAD LIMIT LIGHTS. (See 2 figure 1-30.)- Two limit lights are installed on the pedestal adjacent to the control switch. These lights indicate that the emergency system has reached the load limit and the airplane should be retrimmed to relieve the loads imposed.

1-117. RUDDERS.

1-118. GENERAL.- A hydraulically-actuated, double split-flap type rudder is hinged to each trim flap. The rudders move with the trim flaps when the flaps are used to trim the airplane but they operate independently of the flaps for directional control of the airplane. The rudders may be used simultaneously for braking purposes in the air. Independent rudder pedals, operating through cable systems, control servo valves which regulate hydraulic pressure to the two hydraulic actuating cylinders at each rudder. Emergency controls for rudder operation are not provided.

1-119. RUDDER CONTROLS.- The rudders are controlled by toe-pedals having fixed heel rests. Preload-spring assemblies return the pedals to neutral and furnish "feel" to rudder operation. Pressure on one rudder pedal opens its corresponding rudder, its surfaces deflecting above and below the trim flap. (See figure 1-29.) The pedals are not interconnected, therefore simultaneous movement of the pedals opens both rudders. The rudders also operate when the pedals are used to apply the brakes.

1-120. TRIM CONTROLS.

1-121. GENERAL.- Roll and pitch trim or a combination of both are accomplished by movement of electrically-operated trim flaps. During take-off and landing it is necessary to use nose-up trim. This is accomplished through the use of the trim flaps. The elevons also are provided with an elevator trim control. During high-speed operation it may become necessary to use more pitch trim than is available from the trim flaps. In this event, the elevons may be trimmed for "elevator" trim to gain additional down-elevator trim. Rudder trim is controlled by dc-operated motors which open and close the rudders. Control switches for trim flaps and rudder trim are located on the pilots' pedestal; a knob for elevon trim control is located on the face of the pilot's control column. (See figures 1-31, 1-32 and 1-33.)

1-122. TRIM FLAP CONTROL SWITCH AND POSITION INDICATORS. (See figure 1-31.)- A spring-loaded switch on the pilots' pedestal has four master and four intermediate positions. The master positions are "NOSE-UP," "NOSE - DOWN," "RIGHT WING DOWN," and "LEFT WING DOWN."

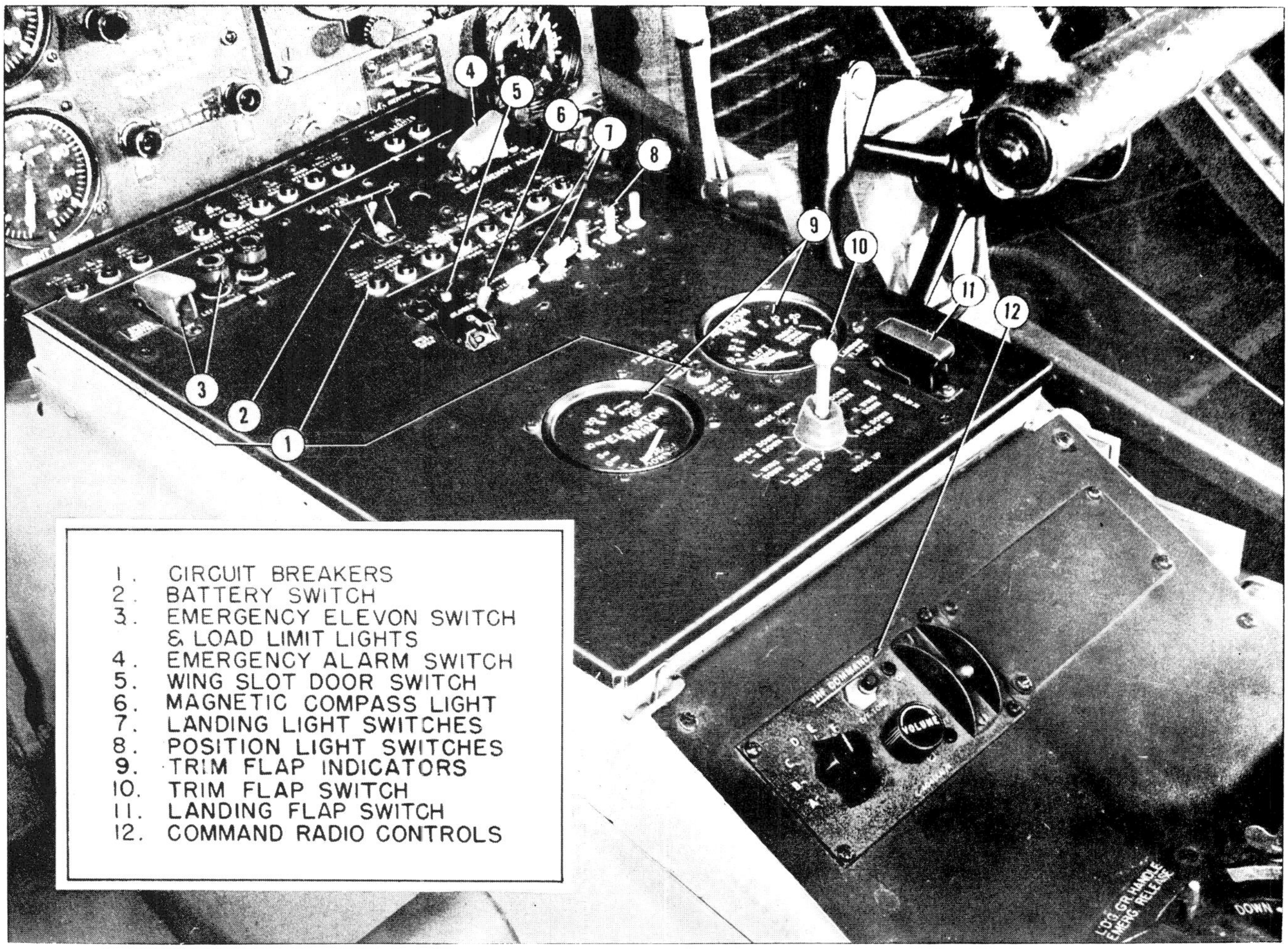

Figure 1-30. Pilot's Pedestal Switch Panel

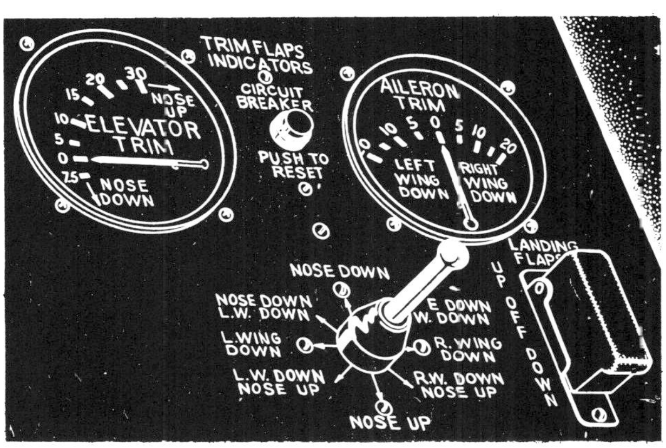

Figure 1-31. Trim Flap Controls

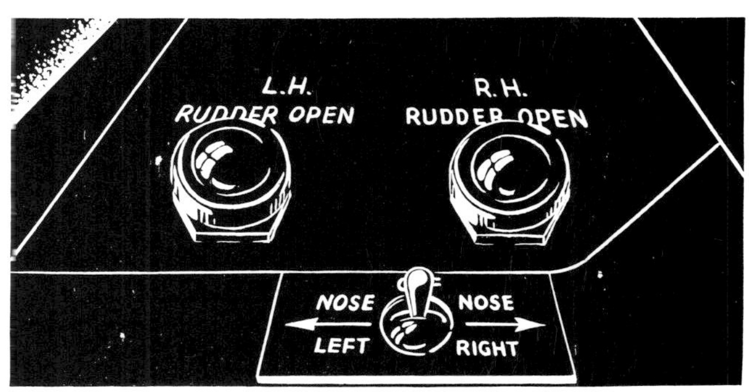

Figure 1-32. Rudder Trim Control (Next to LG Control Handle)

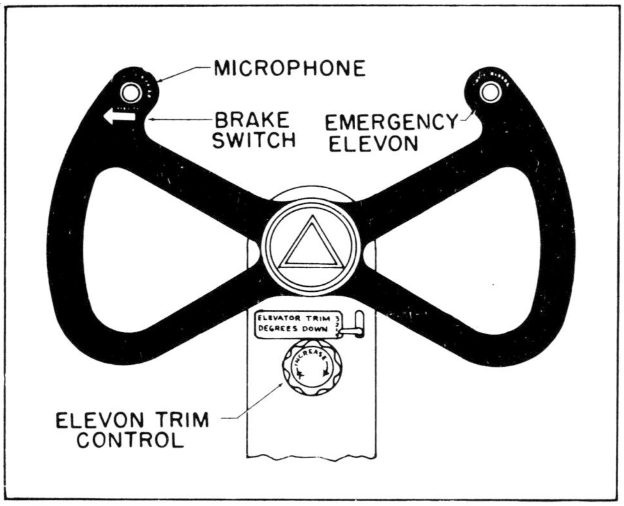

Figure 1-33. Elevon Trim Control

The four intermediate positions provide combinations of trim. Two indicators, for elevator and aileron trim, are located on the pedestal just forward of the control switch. These indicators are not calibrated in degrees of trim.

1-123. RUDDER TRIM CONTROL SWITCH AND INDICATOR LIGHTS. (See figure 1-32.)- A two-position, spring-loaded switch controls the rudders for directional trim. To obtain trim the switch must be held to the position desired, "NOSE LEFT" or "NOSE RIGHT." Two lights adjacent to the switch indicate which rudder is open. A rudder may be returned to neutral by holding the switch to the opposite trim position until the rudder open light goes out, then allowing the switch to return to the center position. As a safety precaution, a landing-gear-operated switch automatically returns the rudder trim to neutral when the landing gear is lowered.

1-124. ELEVON TRIM CONTROL KNOB. (See figure 1-33.)- A knob on the face of the pilot's control column provides "elevator" trim of the elevon by changing the neutral position of the control force bellows linkage.

1-125. LANDING FLAPS.

1-126. GENERAL.- The landing flaps are operated by an ac motor-driven gear-box assembly, through a series of torque tubes and universal joints. A master control switch is located on the pilots' pedestal. Two ac motors normally drive the gear-box assembly to operate the flaps. In the event that one of these motors should fail, the flaps may be operated by the other motor.

1-127. LANDING FLAP NORMAL CONTROL SWITCH AND POSITION INDICATOR. (See 11 figure 1-30 and 25 figure 1-34.)- The landing flap control switch located on the pedestal within reach of either pilot has "UP," "OFF," and "DOWN" positions. Flap movement can be stopped at any position by returning the switch to the "OFF" position. A flap position indicator is located in the lower right corner of the instrument panel.

1-128. EMERGENCY LANDING FLAP CONTROL.

1-129. GENERAL.- The landing flap gear-box assembly is driven by two ac motors having integral brake assemblies which hold the motors when the electric power is off. When the control switch is "OFF" the brakes are set, thus holding the flaps in position. The gear box arrangement is such that the two

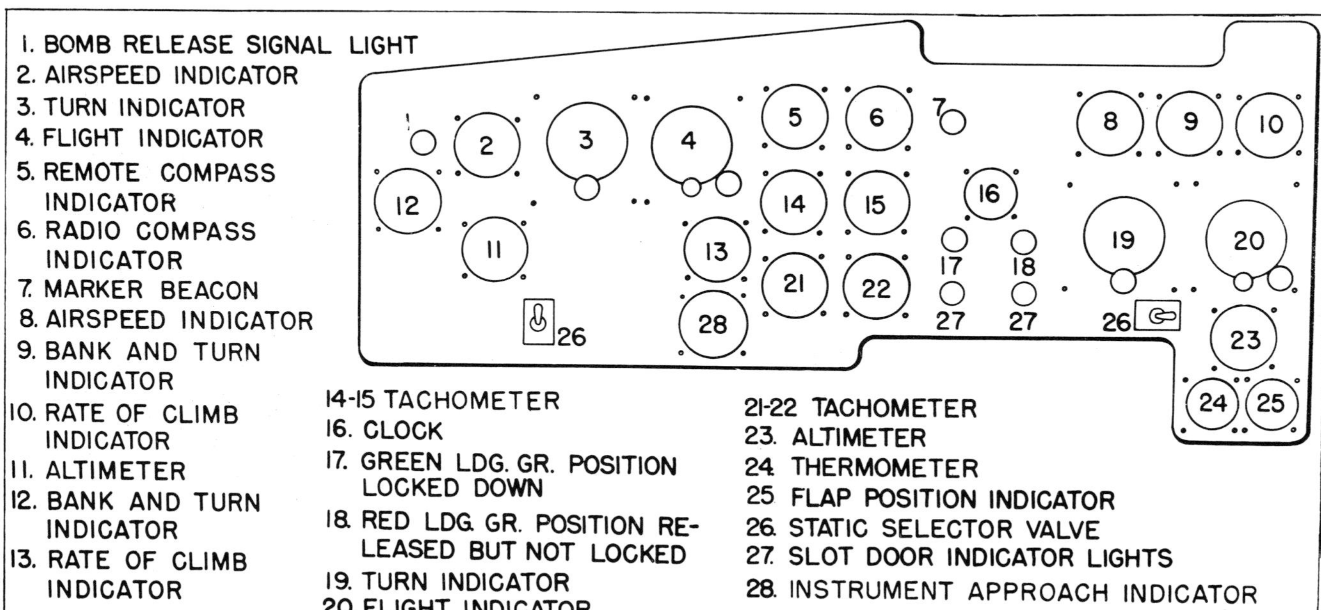

Figure 1-34. Pilot's Instrument Panel

motors operate the flaps through differential gearing. Because of this arrangement, both motors must be operating, or the brake on one engaged, in order to move the flaps. Individual motor switches and an indicator light are installed on the flap power unit to afford control if one motor should fail. A reset handle is located on the side of the flap unit so that the unit may be re-engaged should an overtravel occur.

1-130. FLAP MOTOR SELECTOR SWITCHES. (See figure 1-35.)- These switches are used to check and determine an inoperative motor. These switches are wired so that they control individual motors. When one switch is turned "OFF" it sets the brake on its respective motor so that the other motor may drive the landing flaps.

1-131. FLAP RESET LEVER AND INDICATOR LIGHT. (See figure 1-35.)- This lever is used to re-engage the power unit in the event of an electrical limit switch failure and subsequent disengagement of the unit by the mechanical stop. The red indicator light shows that the flaps are at one extreme of travel. Before attempting to reset the unit, the pilots' switch must be moved to the opposite position causing the light to go out. When this is done the motors will be operating in the proper direction and the unit may be reset by moving the lever outboard as far as possible and then returning it to the inboard position.

1-132. WING SLOT DOORS.

1-133. GENERAL.- A three-position switch permits manual or automatic control of the opening or closing of the wing slot doors in each wing. A hydraulic cylinder in each wing furnishes the power to actuate the doors. Hydraulic fluid to the cylinders is controlled by a solenoid-operated valve. Spring-bungees hold the doors open and also open them in the event of a hydraulic failure. Normally the solenoid valve is

Figure 1-35. Landing Flap Power Unit (Aft Gunner's Compartment)

energized and consequently the doors remain closed. When the circuit to the solenoid is broken, the hydraulic power is cut off, allowing the spring-bungees to open the doors. Automatic control of the doors is accomplished through aerodynamic pressure switches, opening and closing the doors at predetermined lift coefficients. Since it is desirable to have the slot doors open during take-off and landing, a landing-gear-acutated switch opens the doors when the gear is down. The hydraulic system is so designed that it is not possible to have failure on one side of the airplane without failure on the other side. Also the aerodynamic switches are interconnected so that pressure change on one wing will result in the operation of the doors in both wings. The manual positions of the pilots' switch by-pass both the aerodynamic switches and the landing gear switch. Should a mechanical failure hold one set of doors open or closed, the pilot can place the doors in the other wing in the same position through the use of the manual positions of the control switch. Lights indicating the open position of the slot doors are installed on the pilots' instrument panel.

1-134. SLOT DOOR CONTROL SWITCH. (See 5 figure 1-30.)- This three-position switch has "OPEN," "CLOSE," and "AUTO." positions. In the automatic position the doors are opened or closed through the medium of aerodynamic pressure switches, and opened by a landing-gear-operated switch. The "OPEN" and "CLOSE" positions afford manual control. As a precaution the switch should always be placed in the "OPEN" position for take-off and landing. In flight the switch should be in the "AUTO." position.

1-135. SLOT DOOR INDICATOR LIGHTS. (See 27 figure 1-34.)- An amber light is provided for each set of slot doors. When the lights are on they indicate that the doors are open.

1-136. AUTOMATIC PILOT.- Not provided.

1-137. LANDING GEAR.

1-138. GENERAL.

1-139. The tricycle landing gear and the landing-gear fairing doors are actuated by ac electric motors. Dual wheels, each equipped with spot-type brakes, are used on each main gear, and a single steerable wheel is used on the nose gear. The landing-gear up and down locks are operated by electric actuators. The fairing door locks are controlled by a cable system connected to the landing-gear control handle. Except for the strut doors, the fairing doors close when the gear is extended. The doors are closed and locked when the gear is retracted and are closed but not locked when the gear is extended. An emergency release system is incorporated in the landing-gear control system whereby the gears can be fully released for emergency lowering. There are no provisions for emergency retraction. A positive locking arrangement prevents inadvertent retraction of the gear when the airplane is on the ground. Air-oil bungees, attached to the gears and to the nose wheel doors, assure engagement of the gears in the down locks for either normal or emergency extension.

1-140. LANDING GEAR EXTENSION AND RETRACTION SYSTEM.

1-141. GENERAL.- Two methods are used to safety the landing gear when the airplane is on the ground. A "trigger" lock, attached to the control handle, must be raised before the handle can be moved to the "UP" position. In addition to the "trigger" lock, a solenoid-operated plunger blocks the movement of the handle when the weight of the airplane is on the gears. An emergency release lever is provided to override the solenoid permitting the handle to be moved. To assure positive engagement of the gears in the down locks, each gear has been equipped with an air-oil bungee.

1-142. LANDING-GEAR CONTROL HANDLE. (See figure 1-36.)- When the airplane is resting on the ground the landing-gear control handle cannot be moved without raising the "trigger" lock and moving the emergency release lever. To do this requires the use of both hands, which reduces the chances of inadvertent retraction while on the ground. For normal extension of the gear, the landing-gear control handle is moved to the "DOWN" position. Movement of the handle to this posi-

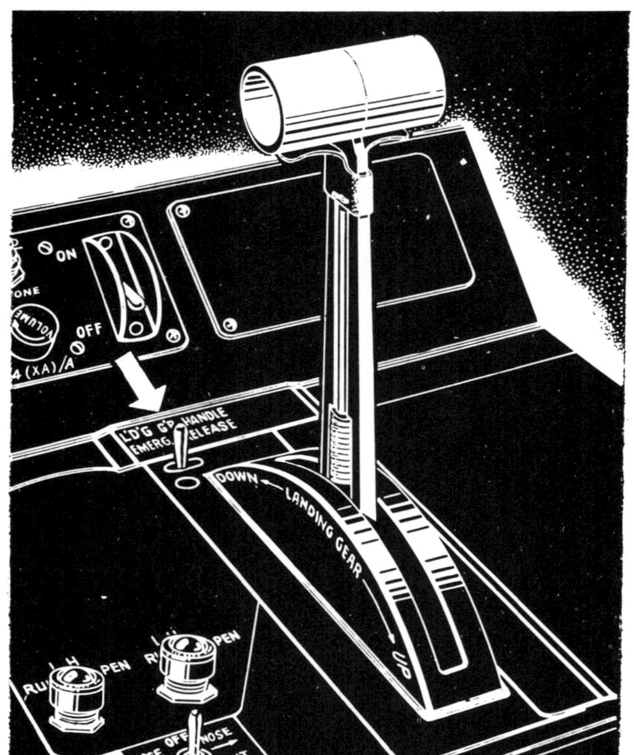

Figure 1-36. Landing Gear Control Handle and Release

tion unlocks the landing-gear door locks by means of a cable system. When the locks are fully open they contact switches which start the landing-gear door motors. Subsequent lowering of the gears and closing of the doors is accomplished by chain-sequence-operation of limit and sequence switches. The down-locks are automatically actuated to the locked positions by entry of lugs attached to the landing gear struts. There is no neutral position of the landing-gear control handle; it will stay in either the "UP" or "DOWN" position. When the control handle is placed in the "UP" position for normal retraction of the gear, it closes switches which actuate the door motors, opening the doors. When the doors are opened, the retraction sequence of the gear into the up-locks and subsequent closing and locking of the fairing doors is automatically accomplished through a series of subsequent switches.

1-143. LANDING-GEAR CONTROL HANDLE EMERGENCY RELEASE LEVER. (See figure 1-36.)- If for any reason the solenoid lock should fail to release the landing gear control handle after the weight of the airplane is off the gears, this emergency release lever will manually move the solenoid so that the control handle can be moved out of the "DOWN" position.

1-144. EMERGENCY LANDING-GEAR RELEASE CONTROL HANDLE. (See figure 1-37.)- A control handle for emergency release of the landing gear is located on the side of the turret structure in the crew's quarters. This handle operates a cable system which unlocks the fairing doors, releases the uplocks, and disengages the clutches of landing-gear actuators allowing the gears to fall of their own weight to a point where the air-oil bungees will force them into the down-locks. The handle operates the same as a mechanics socket ratchet handle. It has a small lever which regulates the direction of ratchet. When this lever is in the "DOWN" position the handle is set to release the gear. Normally the handle hangs downward and by raising it up and down in five 90° movements the gears will be fully released. Once this system is used the normal control handle should be left in the "DOWN" position and no attempt should be made to retract the gear. A pointer operated by movement of the handle indicates the "GEAR LOCKED" and "GEAR UNLOCKED" condition. When this system is operated, it destroys the normal operational sequence timing and the landing-gear system must be reset by the ground crew to restore it to normal operating condition.

1-145. LANDING-GEAR INDICATOR LIGHTS. (See 17 and 18 figure 1-34.)- Two push-to-test lights, one red and one green, are located at the center of the instrument panel. The red light is on when the gears are not in the locks. The green light is on when all gears are in the down-locks. Both lights are out when the gears are up and locked.

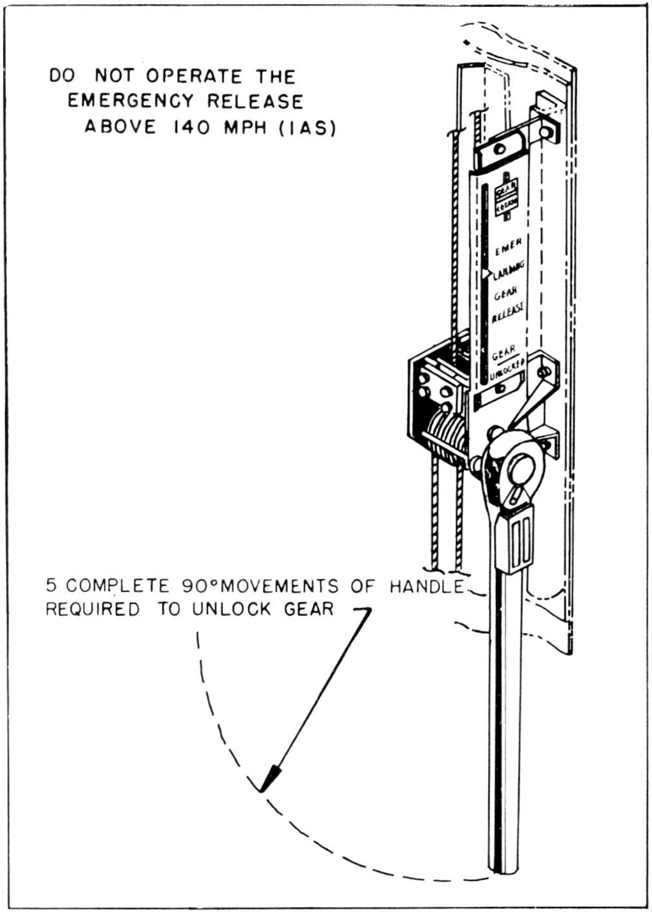

Figure 1-37. Emergency Landing Gear Release (On Side of Center Turret Structure)

1-146. LANDING-GEAR BUNGEE SYSTEM.- Each main gear is equipped with two bungees, the nose gear with one, and the forward and aft nose gear doors each with one. The bungees operate under constant air-oil pressure in the systems. As the landing gear extends, approaching the down-locks, air-oil pressure forces the bungee cylinders against the gears. Theoretically the systems should not have to be recharged as action of the gear, as it is retracted, automatically restores the pressure in the bungee systems. Each bungee pressure gage, however, should be checked before flight. Each main gear bungee should have 900 psi air pressure, the nose gear bungee should have 400 psi air pressure and each nose gear door bungee bottle 1000 psi. (See 3, 18, and 30 figure 1-2.)

1-147. NOSE-WHEEL-STEERING SYSTEM.

1-148. GENERAL.- The nose wheel on this airplane is equipped with a "steer-damp" unit which permits the nose wheel to swivel when the airplane is turned, or allows controlled steering of the wheel through an arc of 98°. The "steer-damp" unit is operated by 3000 psi hydraulic pressure for nose-wheel steering. The pressure is supplied by the brake and steering hydraulic system. Hydraulic pressure to the steering unit is controlled by a solenoid-operated valve, operated by a "trigger" switch on the NOSE WHEEL STEERING AND PARKING BRAKE HANDLE. The control handle is used to turn the nose wheel and also to set the parking brakes.

1-149. NOSE-WHEEL-STEERING CONTROL HANDLE AND SWITCH. (See 2 figure 1-23.)- The steering control handle is located to the left of the pilot. After actuating the steering-control switch, any movement of the handle to the left or right will result in proportional movement of the nose wheel. This switch is located on the control handle so that when the handle is held, the switch is under the forefinger. When the switch is actuated, hydraulic pressure is released to the steering unit so that turning the control handle will turn the wheel. This switch also actuates the main-gear-brake solenoid valve so that pressure on the rudder pedals will apply the brakes. The handle is connected to the steering unit on the nose gear through mechanical linkage. The parking brakes also are operated by this handle.

1-150. BRAKES.

1-151. GENERAL.- Each main-gear wheel is equipped with dual spot-type brakes. The brakes are power operated with hydraulic pressure furnished by the brakes and nose-wheel-steering hydraulic system. Power brake valves, connected to the rudder pedal torque tubes, are operated by normal movement of the rudder pedals. A solenoid-operated valve in the pressure line leading to the brake valves prevents the application of the brakes when the rudders are operated. This solenoid valve is controlled by any one of three switches: one on the steering and parking brake handle, and one on each of the pilots' control wheels. The rudders are operated each time the brakes are applied. An emergency air-brake system is also provided.

1-152. BRAKE CONTROL SWITCHES. (See figure 1-13.)- To secure braking action, press and hold one of the three BRAKE switches, then depress the rudder pedals. A switch should be actuated before the pedals are depressed so that the brakes may be applied gently. If the pedals are depressed first, hydraulic pressure will be free to apply the brakes immediately upon movement of a switch. This will result in abrupt braking action.

1-153. EMERGENCY AIR BRAKES.

1-154. GENERAL.- The emergency air-brake system uses a working air pressure of 1500 psi. The air storage bottle is located in the nose-wheel well and contains sufficient air pressure for four complete actuations of the brakes. (See 20 figure 1-2.)

1-155. EMERGENCY AIR-BRAKE CONTROL LEVERS. (See 1 figure 1-23.)- Two control levers are located overhead between the pilots. Differential and metered pressure is obtained with the use of the two control levers. After operating the brakes the levers will return to the up (off) position. Avoid abrupt operation of the levers.

1-156. FIRE EXTINGUISHER SYSTEMS.

1-157. GENERAL.- A methyl bromide fire extinguisher system is provided for the engine sections, and a carbon dioxide system for protection of the A.P.U.'s. The engine section fire extinguisher is capable of combating two fires on each side of the airplane. The A.P.U. system has only one discharge available.

1-158. ENGINE SECTION FIRE EXTINGUISHER SYSTEM.

1-159. GENERAL.- The engine section fire extinguisher system consists of two equal parts, one for each side of the airplane. Each part is capable of fighting two independent fires, at different times, in any zone. The airplane is divided into eight zones, one zone for each engine, numbered from left to right. (See figure 1-38.) The controls are located at the engineer's station. Heat detector lights are installed near each throttle to indicate a rise in temperature in the engine compartment.

1-160. FIRE DETECTOR INDICATOR LIGHTS. (See 22 figure 1-12.)- Fire detectors are installed in each engine bay to indicate a fire. If a fire should occur, the detectors will light a lamp on the engineer's fire extinguisher panel and the panel behind the throttles. (See paragraph 1-163.)

1-161. FIRE DETECTOR SYSTEM TEST SWITCHES. (See figure 1-38.)- Two spring-loaded test switches are provided for testing the fire detector systems. When a switch is held to the "TEST" position, it causes direct current to flow through the detector system, heating the detector units to simulate a fire condition. The indicator lights should glow within 15 seconds of closing of the test switch if the system is functioning properly.

1-162. FIRE EXTINGUISHER DISCHARGE SWITCHES. (See figure 1-38.)- The zone selector switch may be turned to any one of the eight fire zones. To combat a fire, this switch must be turned to the affected zone, as indicated by the fire detector light, before operating a discharge switch. A discharge switch is provided for each side of the airplane. The discharge switches are spring-loaded to the off position. The up position, releases agent for a first fire and the down position releases agent for a second fire.

1-163. HEAT DETECTOR LIGHTS. (See 1 figure 1-16.)- One row of amber and one row of red indicator lights are installed on a panel in back of the engineer's throttle quadrant. The lights indicate excessive engine compartment temperatures. An amber light indicates an excessive temperature in

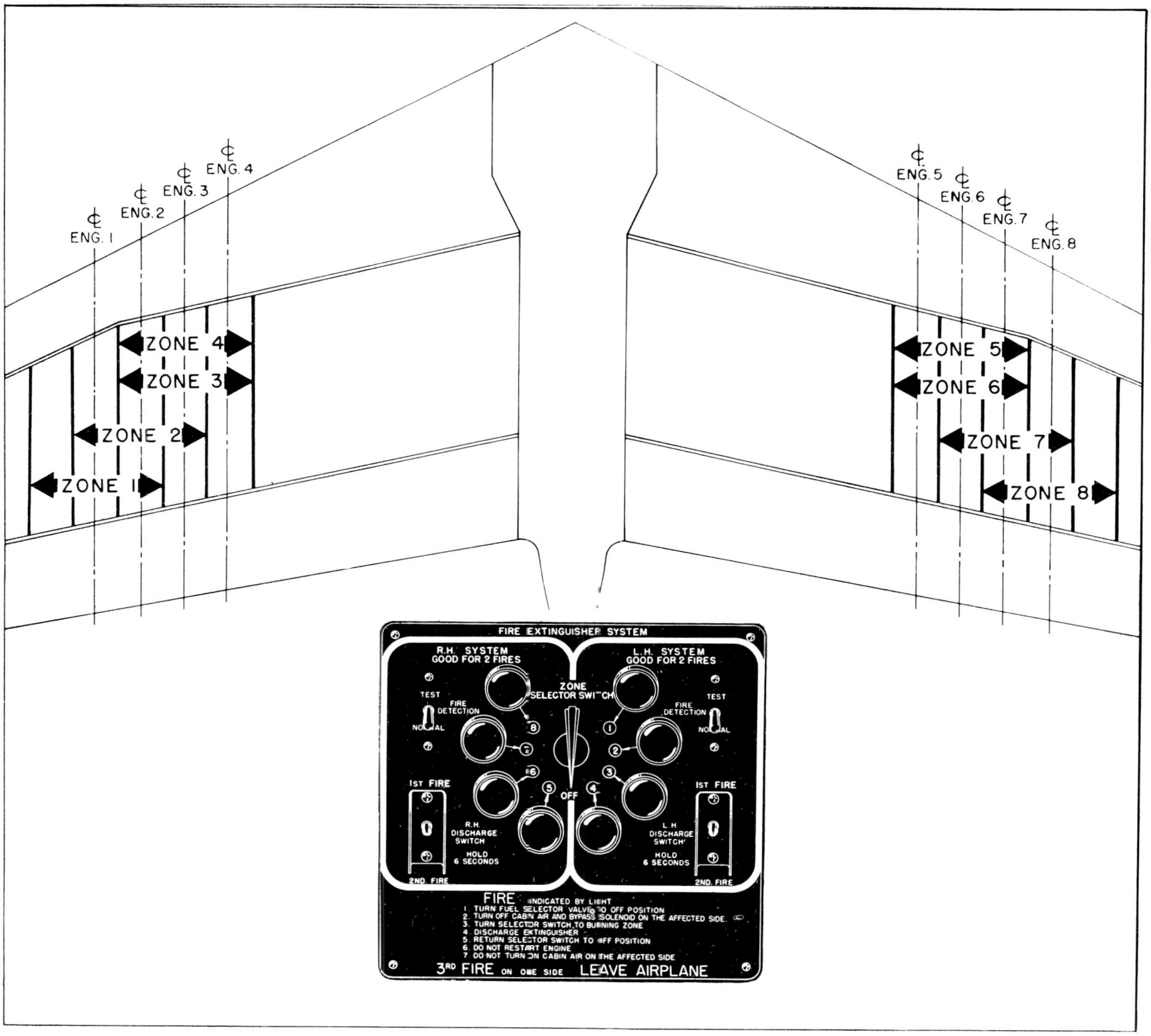

Figure 1-38. Fire Extinguisher Control Zones

the aft engine compartment, and power on that engine should be decreased until the light goes out. A red light indicates a fire condition in the forward engine compartment, and that engine should be shut off immediately and the fire detector lights observed for further indication of a fire before the extinguisher is discharged.

1-164. A.P.U. FIRE EXTINGUISHER SYSTEM.

1-165. GENERAL.- A single-discharge carbon dioxide system is provided for fire control in the A.P.U. compartments.

1-166. INDICATOR LIGHTS. (See figure 1-39.)- One fire indicator light is provided for each A.P.U. They are red lights having conventional push-to-test jewels.

1-167. DISCHARGE SWITCH. (See figure 1-39.)- This is a spring-loaded, double-throw switch. When held to the on position for six seconds, agent will be discharged to the respective A.P.U. compartment.

1-168. INSTRUMENTS.

1-169. GENERAL.

1-170. All gyro instruments are electrically-driven. The fuel level indicators are selsyn operated instruments. Fuel and oil pressure instruments are actuated by fluid pressure transmitters.

Figure 1-39. A.P.U. Fire Extinguisher Control Panel

1-171. STATIC PRESSURE SELECTOR VALVES.

1-172. The pilot and copilot are each furnished with a STATIC PRESSURE SELECTOR VALVE that is operated by a toggle-type lever. (See 26 figure 1-34.) The "AIRSPEED TUBE" position selects static air from the pitot tubes and the "ALTERNATE SOURCE" position selects static air from bomb bay 4 for the pilot and bomb bay 5 for the copilot. The navigator does not have an alternate source of static air.

1-173. PITOT TUBE HEATERS.

1-174. The pitot tube heads and the control bellows incorporate electrical heating elements. A PITOT AND CONT. BELLOWS HEATER switch on the engineer's upper electrical control panel controls direct current to the heaters. (See figure 1-10.)

1-175. THERMOMETERS.

1-176. A free air thermometer is located on the engineer's, pilots' and navigator's instrument panels. The thermometers operate on 28v dc, actuated by resistance bulbs. The engineer's thermometer is used to indicate cabin temperature, and the pilots' and navigator's thermometers indicate free air temperature. (See 11 figure 1-12, 24 figure 1-34, and figure 4-6.)

1-177. MAGNETIC COMPASS.

1-178. A magnetic compass is installed on the window frame in front of the copilot. (See 7 figure 1-23.)

1-179. MISCELLANEOUS.

1-180. GENERAL.

1-181. Miscellaneous stowed equipment is located on the general arrangement diagram. (see 5 figure 1-2.) This equipment includes spare lamps, limiters, jack pads, mooring equipment and airplane reference material.

1-182. DATA CASES.

1-183. One data case is located next to the pilot and another at the navigator's station. A flight report holder is installed on the structure between the pilots.

1-184. HAND FIRE EXTINGUISHERS.

1-185. One hand-operated carbon dioxide fire extinguisher is clipped to the nacelle wall at the radio operator's station and a second extinguisher is located on the aft side of the center turret structure in the crew's quarters.

1-186. OPERATIONAL EQUIPMENT.

1-187. GENERAL.

1-188. Descriptions and pertinent operating instructions for the following listed equipment are included in Section IV:

Oxygen Equipment
Crew Nacelle Heat, Vent, and Pressurizing System
Suit Heater Equipment
Radio Equipment
Gyro Flux-Gate Compass
Driftmeter
Bombing Equipment

This airplane has not been furnished with gunnery equipment, and wing anti-icing systems are not used.

PILOTS NOTES

SECTION II

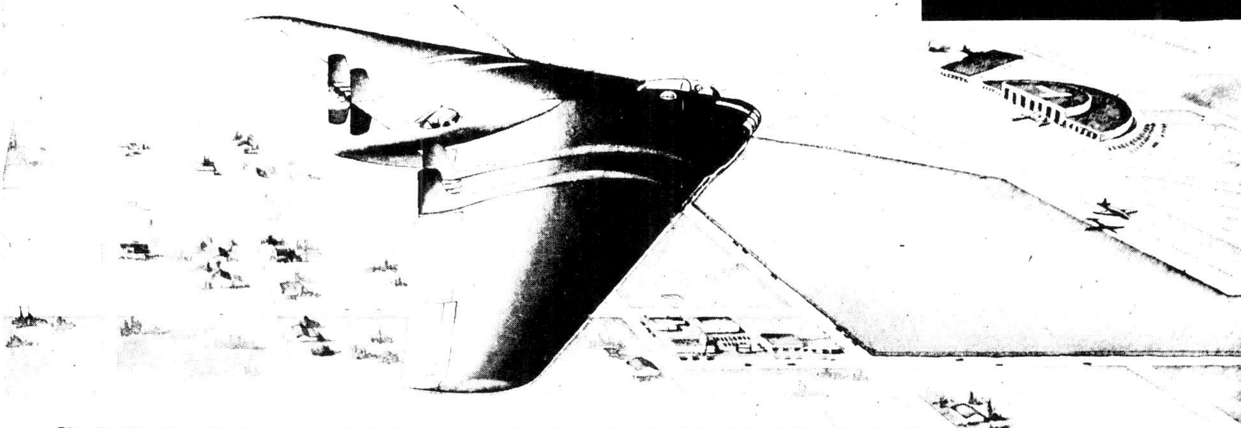

NORMAL OPERATING INSTRUCTIONS

2-1. BEFORE ENTERING THE AIRPLANE.

2-2. RESTRICTIONS.

2-3. The following limitations and restrictions are subject to change, and the latest service directives and orders must be consulted.

2-4. PROHIBITED MANEUVERS.- All acrobatics are prohibited.

2-5. LANDING GEAR.

a. Avoid sharp turns which produce high side loads when taxiing at weights in excess of 155,000 lbs.

b. Do not lower the landing gear above 175 mph or exceed this speed on take-off until the gear is up and the doors are closed.

2-6. LANDING LIGHTS.- Do not extend the landing lights above 175 mph.

2-7. LOADING CONDITIONS.

2-8. Determine the gross weight and balance of the airplane. Complete weight and balance charts locating the center of gravity under various load conditions are supplied with the airplane. The design gross weight and maximum alternate weight is 213,500 lbs. Maximum weight for landing is 146,548 lbs. Refer to the Handbook of Weight and Balance Data, AN 01-1B-40.

2-9. EXTERIOR INSPECTION.

Pilots

a. See that the wheels are chocked and check the condition of the tires and shock struts.

b. Bomb Bay Doors - Closed.

Engineer

a. See that the engine sections have been properly inspected.

b. Check for servicing of fuel tanks, oil tanks, hydraulic reservoirs, landing gear bungee air bottles, emergency air brake bottle, and the nose steering and brake accumulator. (See figure 1-2.)

WARNING

Be absolutely sure that the fuel system manifold has been properly purged of air after filling of the fuel tanks. If this is not done, use of the manifold line to supply fuel to an engine may result in engine failure.

Pilots

c. Check all seams for apparent fluid leaks.

d. See that the wings are free of oil or heavy accumulations of dust.

e. See that ground crew personnel are stationed at the nose gear with earphones and microphones plugged in.

f. Check the control surfaces for damaged fabric or skin.

g. Check Form 1A.

Engineer

c. See that the A.P.U.'s have been serviced with fuel and oil.

d. See that all dust covers are removed.

e. See that the area behind the airplane is clear, and that adequate fire extinguishing equipment is available.

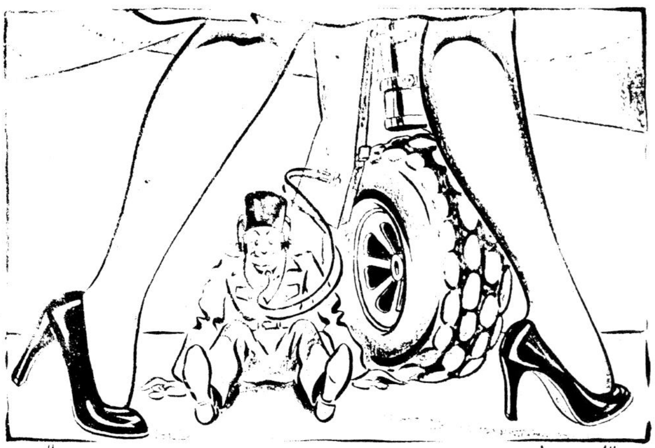

"GROUND CREW TO ENGINEER — BLONDE AT ONE O'CLOCK!"

Ground Crew Interphone In Use

Figure 2-1. Entrance

2-10. ENTRANCE TO THE AIRPLANE.

2-11. The entrance hatch is located in the bottom center of the crew nacelle and the entrance ladder is normally stowed in the crew's quarters. (See figure 2-1.)

2-12. ON ENTERING THE AIRPLANE.

Pilots

a. Visually check the upper escape hatch on entering the airplane.

NOTE

> The brakes cannot be set until ac power is on the airplane. The flight surfaces cannot be operated until at least one engine on each side of the airplane is operating.

b. Control Bellows- Engaged. (See figure 1-28.)

c. Battery Switch - Check "ON." (See 2 figure 1-30.)

Engineer

a. Fuel Control Switches - "OFF" and "CLOSED." (See figure 1-26.)

b. Hydraulic Override Switch - "OFF." (See 16 figure 1-12.)

c. Battery Switch - "OFF." (See figure 1-10.)

Pilots	Engineer
d. See that the circuit breakers on the pedestal are on. (See 1 figure 1-30.)	d. External dc Power - Have ground crew connect. (See 13 figure 1-2.)
	e. Ground Crew Interphone Switch - "ON." (See 20 figure 1-12.)
f. Check interphone.	f. Check interphone.
g. Check condition of instruments, indicator and warning lights.	g. Circuit Breakers - All "ON," except PITOT AND CONTROL BELLOWS HEATER. (See figures 1-10 and 1-26.)
h. Check Landing Gear Indicator Lights - Green light on. (See 17 figure 1-34.)	h. Check instruments, indicator and warning lights.
i. Gyro - "UNCAGED." (See figure 1-34.)	i. Check fuel level indicators against known fuel quantities.
j. Static Pressure Selector Valve "AIRSPEED TUBE." (See 26 figure 1-34.)	j. Fuel Counter Indicators - Set as necessary. (See paragraph 1-98.)
k. Test operate the crew's alarm bell. (See 4 figure 1-30.)	k. Ring Bus-Ext. Pwr. Circuit Breaker - "ON." (See figure 1-5.)
l. Throttle Levers - Retard position.	l. Ring Bus Relays - "OFF." (See figure 1-5.)
m. Throttle Disengage Levers - Automatic position.	m. Exciter Field Switches - "OFF." (See figure 1-5.)
n. Cabin Air - LH and RH switches "OFF." (See figure 4-3.)	n. Load Off Switches - Trip momentarily. (See figure 1-5.)
	o. A.P.U. Relay Switches - "OFF." (See figure 1-5.)
	p. Motor-Generator Switches - "OFF." (See figure 1-8.)
	NOTE External ac power is used principally for ground crew operations.
	q. Fire Detector System - Test. (See figure 1-38.)
	r. Shut-Off By-Pass Valve - "OPEN." (See figure 1-10.)
	s. Battery Heater Switch - "OFF." (See figure 1-10.)
	t. Heat Detector Switch - "ON."

2-13. STARTING A.P.U.'s (Engineer).

a. Fire Control.- Observe indicator lights while starting A.P.U.'s.

b. Start one A.P.U. at a time. (See figure 1-5.)

c. Fuel System and Oil Temperature Switches.- "ON."

d. Fuel Pump Switch.- On "FUEL PUMP."

e. Magneto Switches.- Both "ON."

f. Ignition (magneto) Lights.- Green lights on.

g. Start Switch.- Hold to start, observe tachometer for start of unit. If unit does not start after cranking for several seconds, use prime.

h. Prime Switch.- Hold to "PRIME" momentarily if necessary.

i. After Start.- Allow unit to operate at 1500 rpm until engine warms up, approximately 3 to 4 minutes minimum.

TAKE-OFF & CLIMB

1. SELECTOR VALVES ON - TANK TO ENGINE & MANIFOLD
2. MAIN TANK PUMPS "ON"
3. B.B. TANK SHUT-OFF VALVES - 2 & 7 OPEN
4. B.B. TANK FUEL PUMPS 2, & 7 ON
5. CROSS-FUEL VALVES-CLOSED
6. MANIFOLD VALVES -CLOSED
7. AUX. TANK VALVES & PUMPS-OFF

LANDING

1. SELECTOR VALVES ON TANK TO ENGINE & MANIFOLD
2. IF FUEL IS LEFT IN AUXILIARY OR BOMB BAY TANKS, USE THAT FUEL ALSO.

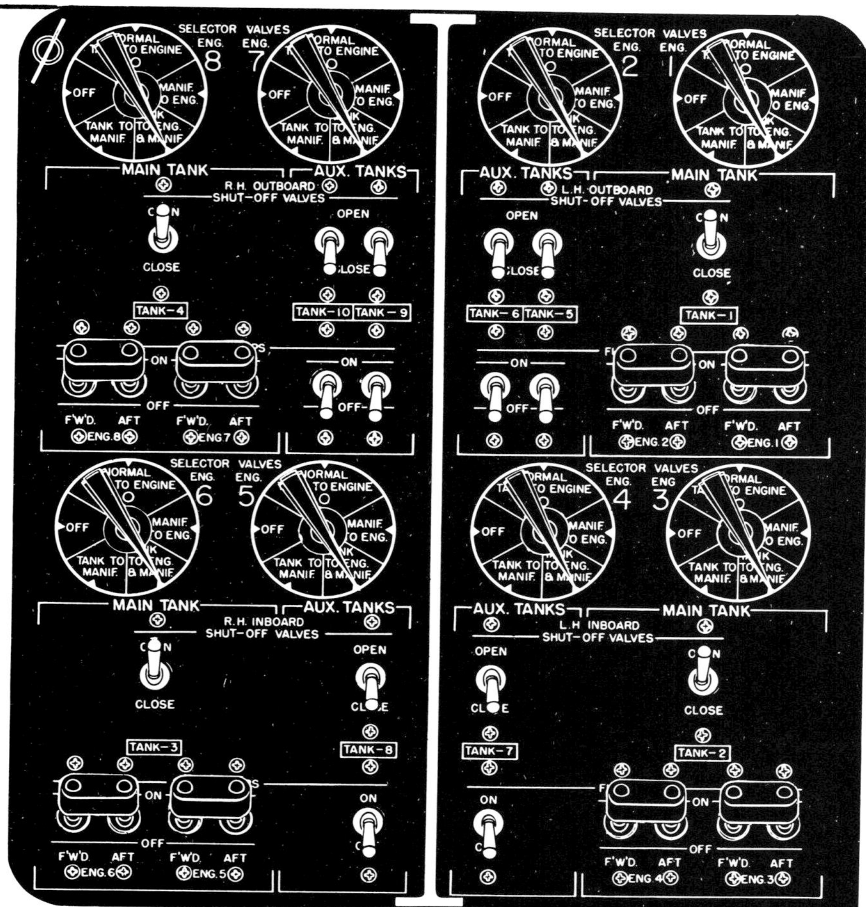

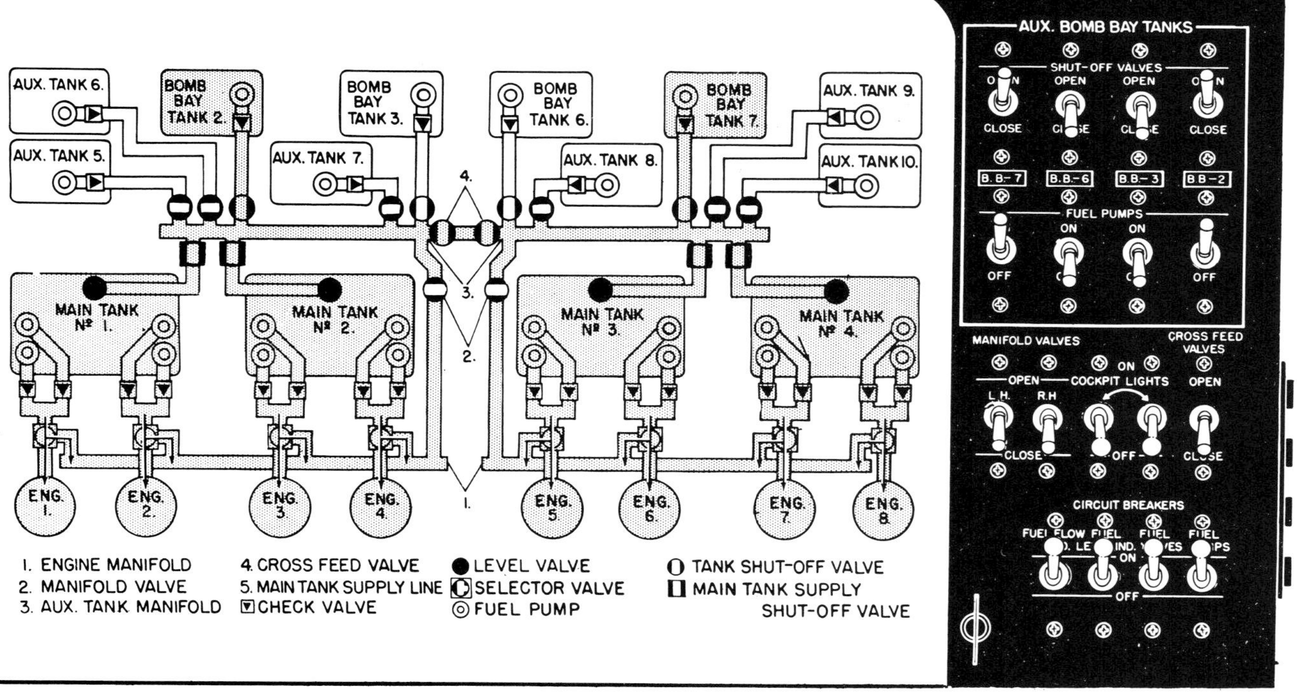

Figure 2-2. Fuel System Management (Sheet 1 of 4 Sheets)

NORMAL

DIAGRAM SHOWS COMPLETE NORMAL FUEL FLOW. THE FOLLOWING IS THE OPERATIONAL SEQUENCE TO BE USED.

1. SELECT "TANK TO ENGINE" FOR EACH ENGINE.
2. TURN ON EACH MAIN TANK PUMP.
3. OPEN EACH AUXILIARY AND BOMB BAY TANK VALVE.
4. OPEN EACH MAIN TANK VALVE.
5. TURN ON THE FUEL PUMPS FOR BOMB BAYS 2 AND 7 AND BOMB BAYS 3 AND 6.
6. WHEN THE BOMB BAY TANKS ARE EMPTY, TURN ON THE FUEL PUMPS FOR AUXILIARY 6 & 9 AND AUXILIARY 5 & 10.
7. WHEN AUXILIARY 5 & 10 ARE HALF EMPTY, TURN ON THE FUEL PUMPS FOR AUXILIARY 7 AND 8.
8. TURN OFF FUEL PUMPS AS THE TANKS EMPTY.

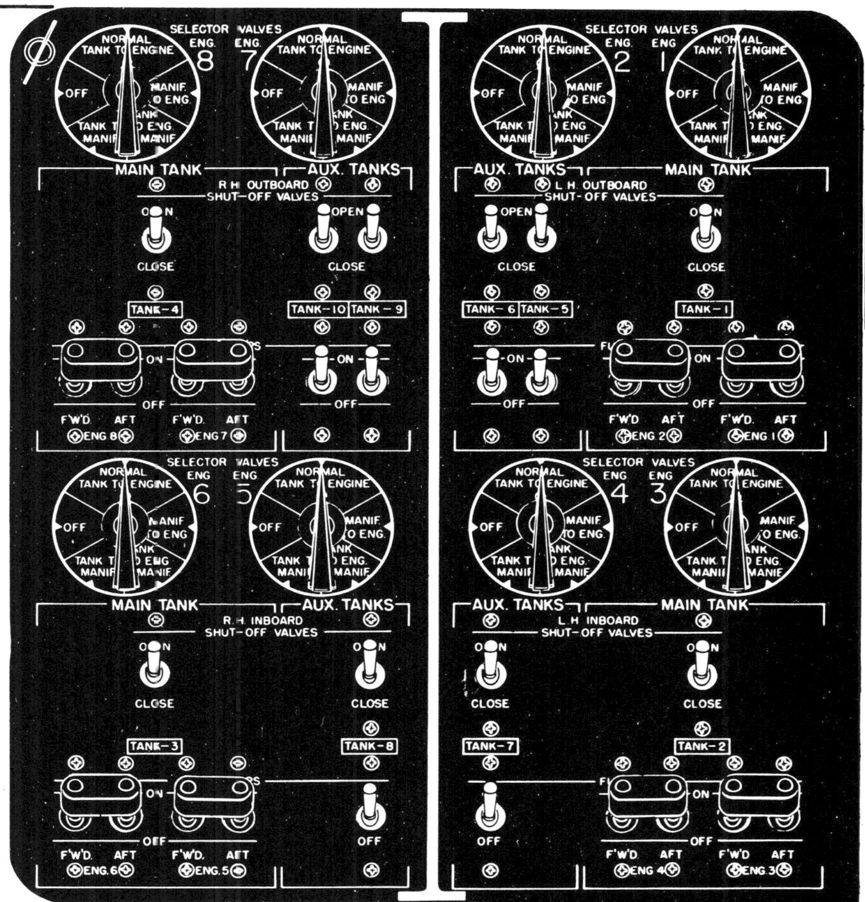

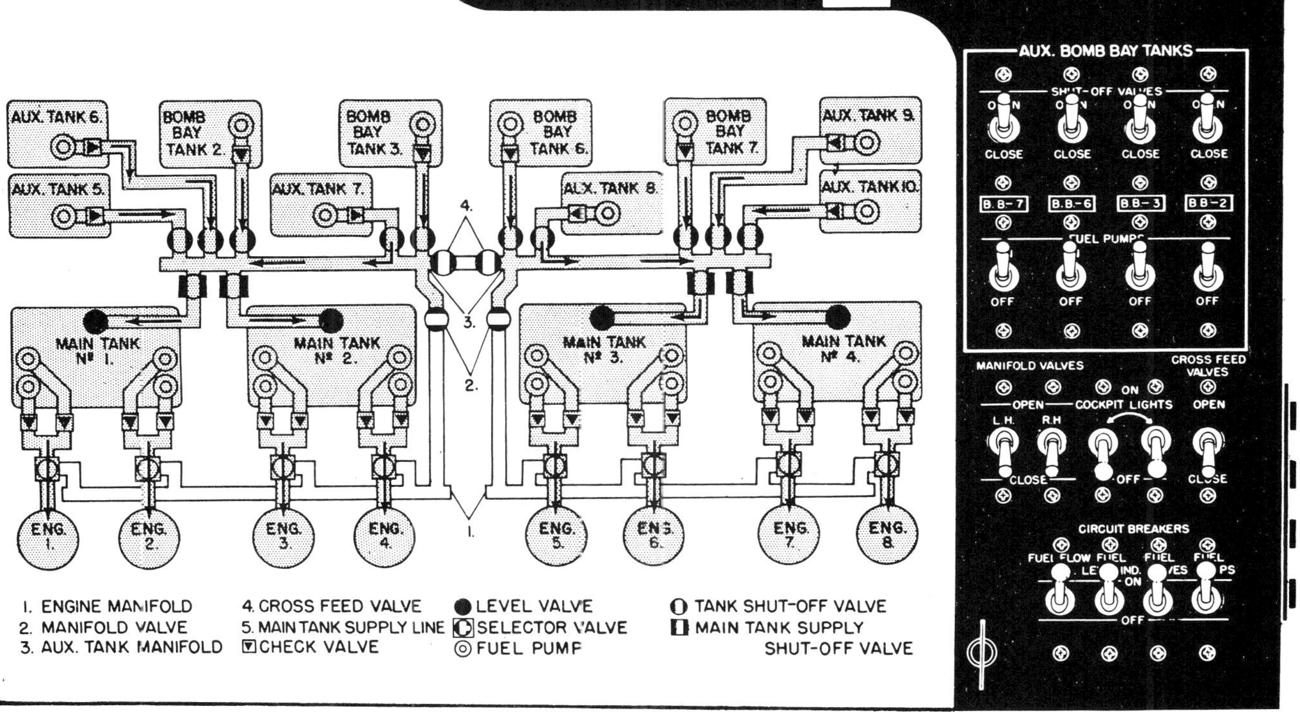

Figure 2-2. Fuel System Management (Sheet 2 of 4 Sheets)

TRANSFER BETWEEN ADJACENT MAIN TANKS

DIAGRAM SHOWS FUEL TRANSFER FROM #1 TANK TO #2 AND #4 TANK TO #3.

1. FOR TANK WHICH IS TO PROVIDE FUEL:
   a. "CLOSE" THE SHUT-OFF VALVE FOR THAT TANK.
   b. SELECT "TANK TO ENGINE AND MANIFOLD" FOR BOTH ENGINES RECEIVING FUEL FROM THAT MAIN TANK.
   c. "OPEN" THE CORRESPONDING MANIFOLD VALVE.
2. FOR TANK WHICH IS TO RECEIVE FUEL:
   a. "OPEN" THE TANK SHUT-OFF VALVE.
   b. SELECT "TANK TO ENGINE".

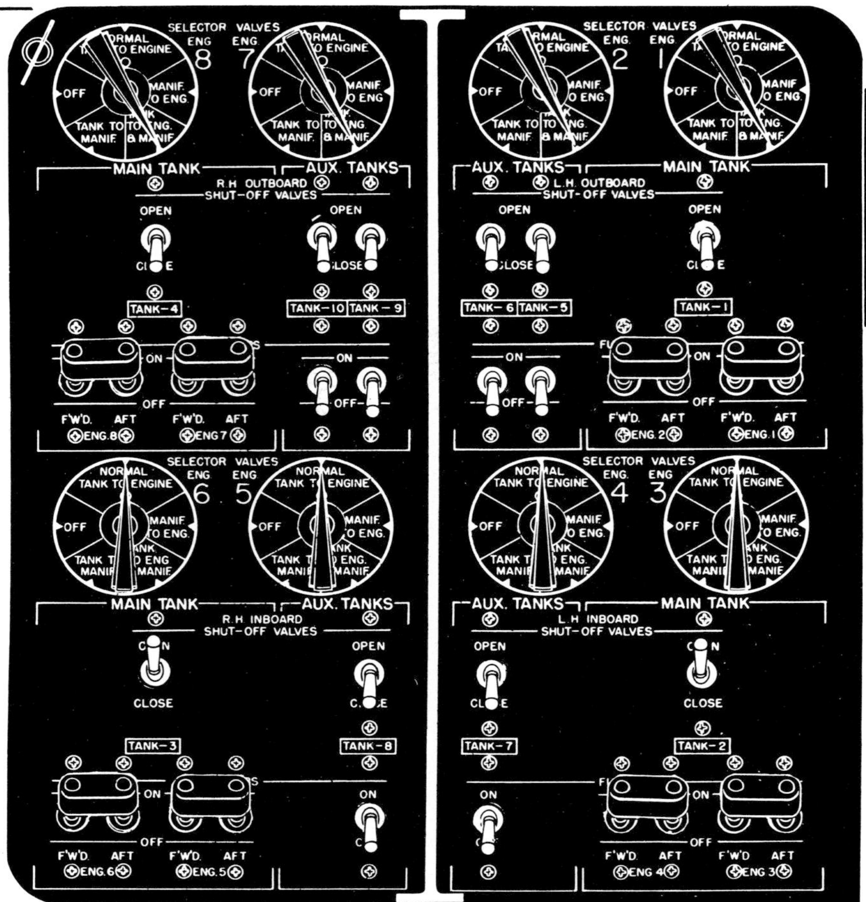

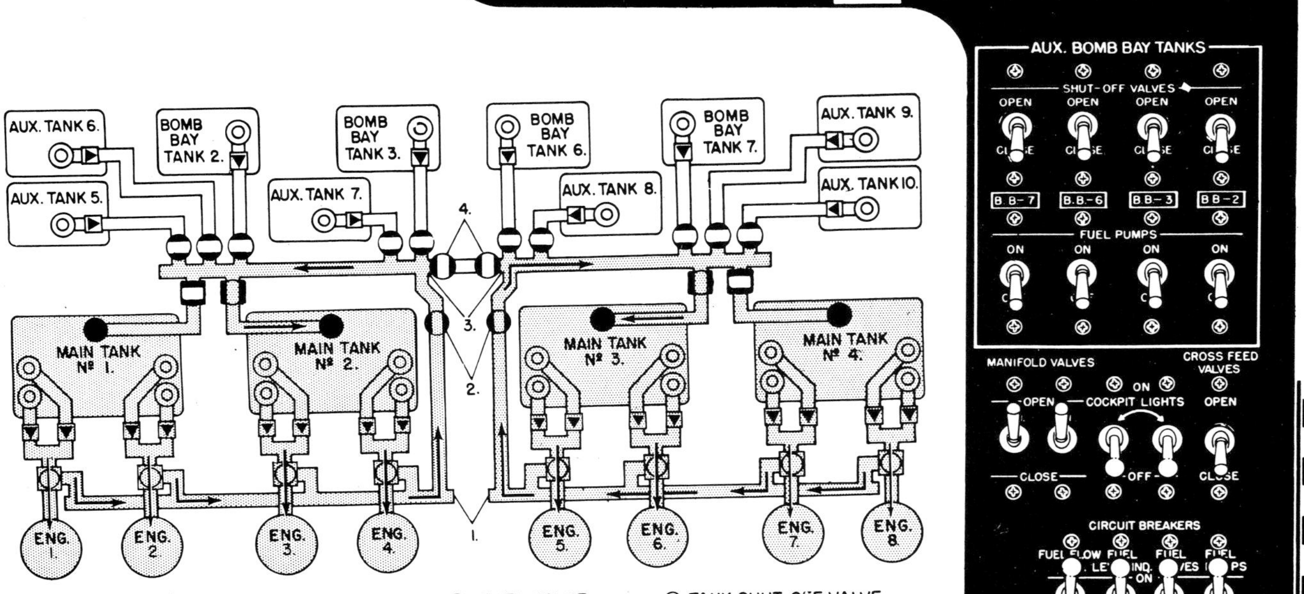

1. ENGINE MANIFOLD
2. MANIFOLD VALVE
3. AUX. TANK MANIFOLD
4. CROSS FEED VALVE
5. MAIN TANK SUPPLY LINE

● LEVEL VALVE
SELECTOR VALVE
CHECK VALVE
◎ FUEL PUMP
TANK SHUT-OFF VALVE
MAIN TANK SUPPLY SHUT-OFF VALVE

Figure 2-2. Fuel System Management (Sheet 3 of 4 Sheets)

MAIN TANK CROSS TRANSFER

DIAGRAM SHOWS FUEL BEING TRANSFERED FROM #1 MAIN TANK TO #3 MAIN TANK.

TO CROSS TRANSFER FUEL BETWEEN ONE OF MAIN TANKS 1 AND 2 AND ONE OF MAIN TANKS 3 AND 4 USE THE FOLLOWING PROCEDURE:

1. "CLOSE" ALL MAIN TANK SHUT-OFF VALVES EXCEPT THE ONE TO THE TANK THAT IS TO RECEIVE FUEL,"OPEN" THAT ONE.
2. FOR THE TANK WHICH IS TO PROVIDE FUEL:
   a. SELECT "TANK TO ENGINE AND MANIFOLD" FOR BOTH ENGINES RECEIVING FUEL FROM THIS MAIN TANK.
   b. "OPEN" THE CORRESPONDING MANIFOLD VALVE.
3. FOR THE TANK WHICH IS TO RECEIVE FUEL:
   a. SEE THAT IT'S SHUT-OFF VALVE IS "OPEN."
   b. "OPEN" THE CROSS-FEED VALVES.

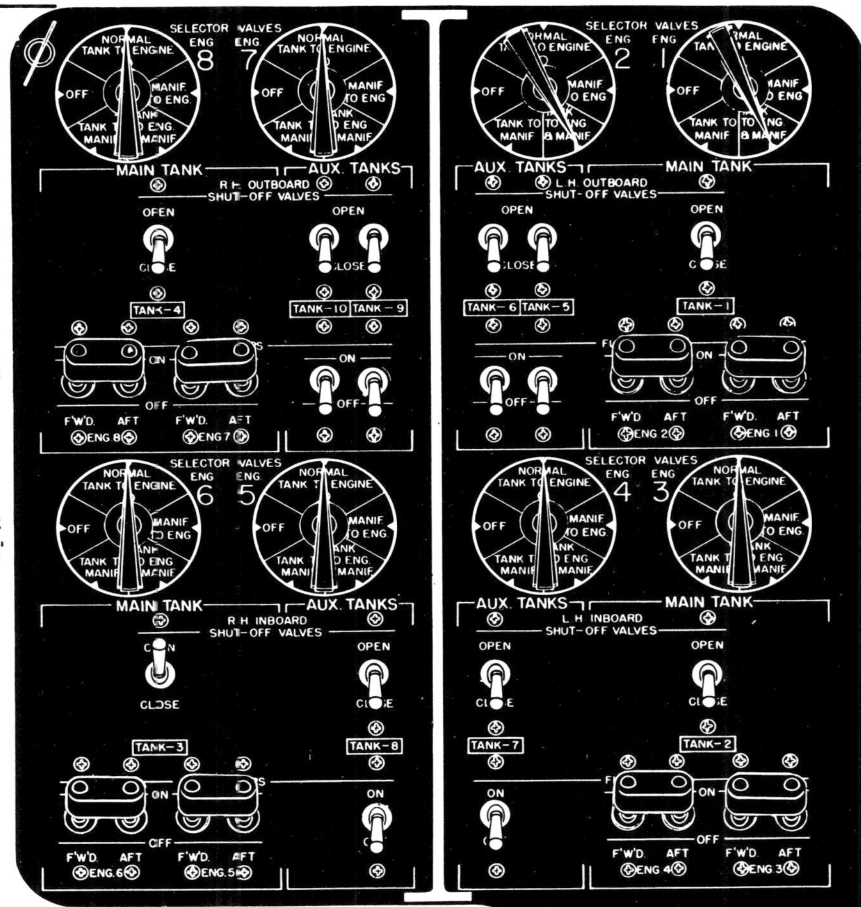

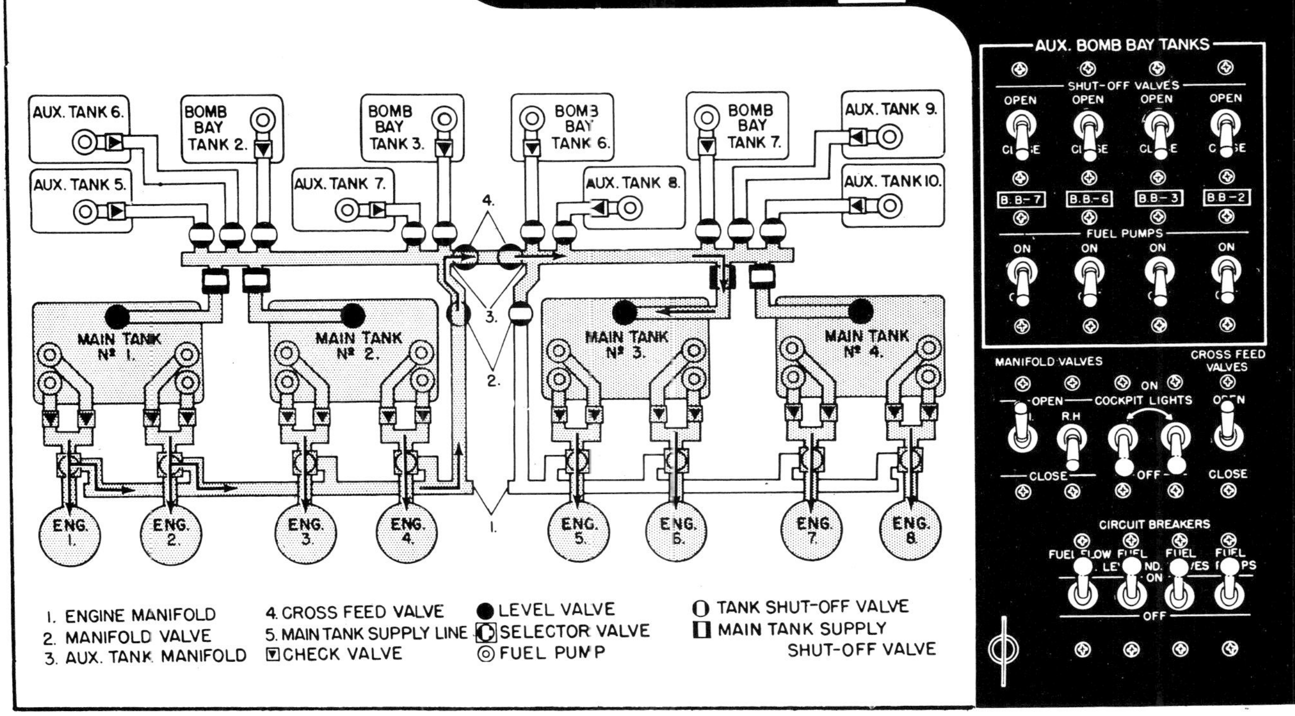

Figure 2-2. Fuel System Management (Sheet 4 of 4 Sheets)

j Speed Control Switch.- Hold to "FULL SPEED" position until unit is operating at 3620 rpm.

k. A.P.U. Cooling Flaps.- Regulate A.P.U. cylinder head temperature as necessary by means of the A.P.U. COOLING AIR VALVE Switch.

l. Exciter Field Switch.- "ON."

NOTE

> Do not throw the exciter field into the alternator circuit at speeds lower than 2600 rpm, as an additional load will be placed on the alternator field causing it to overheat.

m. Frequency.- Check for 420 cycles. Increase or decrease speed of unit to obtain this reading.

n. Voltage.- 208v. Adjust "VOLTAGE" rheostat to obtain correct voltage.

o. A.P.U. Relay Switch.- Respective switch "ON."

p. Load On Switch.- Hold to "ON" momentarily.

q. Ring Bus Relay Switches.- If the left-hand A.P.U. has been started, turn "ON" relay A. If right-hand is started, turn "ON" relay C.

NOTE

> Do not close relay switches B and D while both A.P.U.'s are operating, as it is not desirable to operate the A.P.U.'s in parallel. If only one A.P.U. is operating, all relay switches must be "ON" so that the one unit can supply ac to the whole airplane.

r. Start the second A.P.U. in the foregoing manner.

s. Paralleling A.P.U.'s.- The A.P.U.'s should not be operated in parallel.

t. Motor-Generators and External dc Power.- Do not start the motor-generators until the engines are all started. Use of the engine starters and the motor-generators at the same time will overload the A.P.U.'s. Leave dc external power on until the motor-generators are started.

PILOTS NOTES

2-14. FUEL SYSTEM MANAGEMENT. (See figure 2-2.)

2-15. Normally fuel from the bomb bay and auxiliary tanks is fed into the main tanks and then directed to the engines. Fuel that is farthest behind the center of gravity is used first. Fuel pumps in tanks supplying fuel must be operating continuously and the main tanks pumps must be on at all times. The fuel usage sequence is as follows: First the bomb bay tanks are used, then auxiliary tanks 6, 9, 5, and 10. When tanks 5 and 10 are one-half empty, auxiliary tanks 7 and 8 are used. As the bomb bay and auxiliary tanks empty, their respective FUEL PUMP and SHUT-OFF VALVE switches should be turned "OFF" and "CLOSED."

Know Your Fuel System

2-16. TAKE-OFF AND CLIMB.

a. Selector Valves.- All on "TANK TO ENGINE AND MANIFOLD."

b. Bomb Bay Tank Shut-Off Valves.- 2, 7, "OPEN."

c. Main Tank Supply Line Shut-Off Valves.- All "OPEN."

d. Fuel Pumps.- "ON" in bomb bay and main tanks.

2-17. NORMAL CRUISE.

a. Selector Valves.- On "TANK TO ENGINE."

b. Use bomb bay tanks first. When they are empty, "OPEN" the tank SHUT-OFF VALVES for auxiliary tanks 6, 9, 5, and 10 and turn "ON" the corresponding fuel pumps.

c. When tanks 5 and 10 are one-half empty, also "OPEN" the SHUT-OFF VALVES for tanks 7 and 8 and turn "ON" their fuel pumps. Tanks 6 and 9 are smaller than 5 and 10 and therefore empty first.

d. As the tanks empty, turn "OFF" their FUEL PUMPS and "CLOSE" the SHUT-OFF VALVES.

2-18. LANDING.- Selector valves on "TANK TO ENGINE AND MANIFOLD." If fuel is left in auxiliary and bomb bay tanks, land using take-off configuration.

2-19. STARTING THE ENGINES.

2-20. STARTING PROCEDURE (Engineer).

a. Refer to Section III for Engine Fire.

b. Fuel Tank Shut-Off Valve Switches. (See figure 2-2.)- "CLOSED."

c. Bearing Temperature Switches. (See figure 1-10.)- As required.

d. Master Throttle Switch. (See figure 1-16.)- Hold to "ADVANCE" until the

Keep Clear of the Intake Ducts

motor-drives stop and then to "RETARD" until the motor-drives stop again. This will locate all motor-drives in the electric retard position at 65% rpm.

e. Throttle Levers.- To be sure that the pilots' throttle levers are in the idle position, manually move one throttle lever in each bank of four until it engages with the pilots' follow-up arm assembly notch. Raise the "trigger" of the throttles so used and return them to the "CLOSED" position.

f. Fuel Selector Valves. (See figure 2-2.)- Turn these switches to "NORMAL TANK TO ENGINE AND MANIFOLD" positions.

g. Fuel Pump Switches. (See figure 2-2.)- Turn "ON" the MAIN TANK PUMPS for the engine to be started.

h. Fire Zone Selector Switch. (See figure 1-38.)- To engine to be started.

i. Starter dc Power.- Check with ground crew.

j. Starter and Ignition Switches. (See figure 1-10.)- Engage both switches, release starter but hold ignition switch on until engine starts. Check the time when switches are engaged.

k. At 6-8% rpm open the throttle to 30-40 psi fuel pressure.

NOTE

> The % rpm tachometers may lag behind the engines. If after about 20 seconds of starter engagement there is no rpm indication, proceed with starting and check the tail pipe temperature gage for start.

l. Tail Pipe Temperature.- Check. It may be necessary to tap the gage lightly to be sure that it is registering.

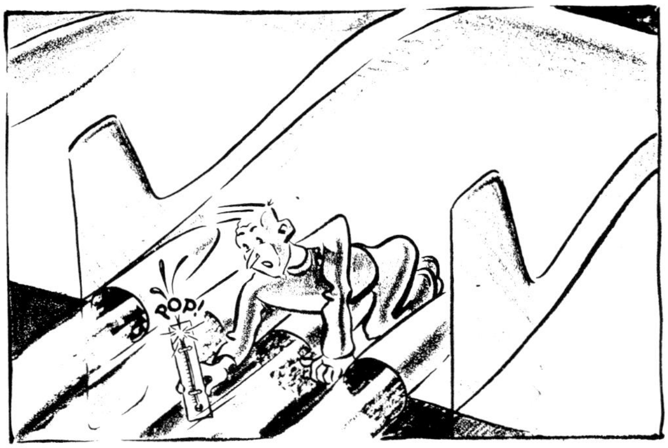

Watch Tailpipe Temperature When Starting

m. After ignition occurs, as indicated by rising of the tail pipe temperature, advance the throttle as rapidly as the tail pipe temperature will allow until the engine reaches about 50% rpm.

NOTE

> The engine installation will cool best at about 50% rpm.

n. Starter and Ignition Switches.- Release the ignition switch and turn "OFF" the starter switch.

o. Tail Pipe Temperature.- A "hot start," defined as a start where the tail pipe temperature rises above 870°C for one minute, must be recorded on Form 1A.

p. THROTTLE LEVER.- Advance the throttle until it engages in the pilots' follow-up arm assembly.

q. The engine should be allowed to operate around 50% while starting the others. Start each engine in turn in accordance with the preceding instructions.

u. Throttle Levers. (See figure 1-16.)- After all engines are started and the throttle levers have been engaged with the notches in the pilots' follow-up arm assemblies, engage each lever with the motor-drive units as follows: Raise one "trigger" to clear the recess in the lever, press down on the other and hold the respective trim switch to "RETARD" until they raise and then drop full down into the notch in the motor-drive bellcrank.

2-21. AFTER ALL ENGINES ARE STARTED.

Pilots	Engineer
a. Parking Brakes - Set.	a. Fire Zone Selector Switch - "OFF."
	b. Main Tank Supply and Bomb Bay Fuel Tank Shut-Off Valve Switches - "OPEN."
	c. Main and Bomb Bay Tanks Fuel Pump Switches - "ON."
	d. Motor-Generators - "ON." Check for 28v and adjust if necessary to obtain correct voltage. (See figure 1-8.)
e. Emergency Elevon Operation - Engage switch and check operation of elevons. (See figure 1-28.)	e. Battery Switch - "ON." (See figure 1-10.)
f. Flight Controls - Check normal operation of all flight controls.	f. Notify ground crew to cut dc external power.
g. Doors and Hatches - Check with crew members to be sure doors and hatches are secure.	g. Hydraulic Power Boost Systems - Check gages for hydraulic pressure. (See 19 figure 1-12.)
h. Radio - Check radio with tower. Check radio compass.	h. Hydraulic Brake and Steering System - Check gage for hydraulic pressure. (See 15 figure 1-12.)
	i. Throttles - About 50% rpm.
	j. Check engine instruments.
k. Check with engineer for taxi O.K.	k. Notify pilot when ready to taxi.

Pilots | Engineer

NOTE

Engine run-up check is generally made at the head of the runway when the engines are advanced for T.O. thrust.

1. Acknowledge engineer and have ground crew remove wheel chocks and disconnect from the interphone circuit.

1. Ground Crew Interphone Switch - "OFF."

2-22. TAXIING INSTRUCTIONS.

2-23. The eight engines consume approximately 25 gallons per minute during ground operation.

CONTROL TOWER TO PILOT——©*?★+≢!!?

Watch Your Wing Tips

2-24. PRECAUTIONS TO BE OBSERVED.

a. Do not turn the nose wheel with the airplane stationary.

b. Avoid sudden turns. Do not force the nose wheel to turn. Use only a follow-up motion of the steering control handle.

c. Do not engage a brake switch while the rudder pedals are depressed. This would apply the brakes abruptly.

d. Do not taxi fast.

2-25. USE OF NOSE WHEEL STEERING AND BRAKES.

2-26. STEERING.- Use a follow-up motion with the handle so as to turn the nose wheel gently. Forcing the nose wheel to turn may result in slippage of the steering linkage.

2-27. BRAKES.- Whenever the trigger switch on the parking brake handle is actuated, or the brake switch on either control wheel is pressed, either pilot may use the rudder pedals to apply the brakes. If the airplane gains excessive speed while taxiing, the pilot may pull the parking brake handle out to apply the brakes. This is suggested because the parking brake meters pressure evenly to the brakes so that the airplane may more readily be slowed or stopped in a straight line.

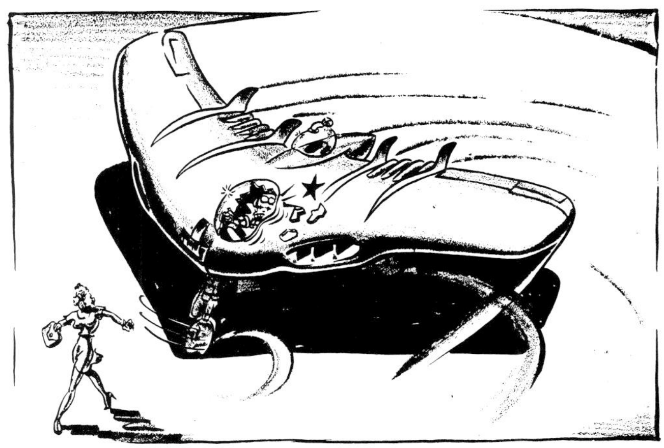

Turn the Airplane Gently

2-28. USE OF THROTTLES FOR TAXIING.

2-29. The pilot should advance the throttles for taxi thrust at "low speed," that is, without the use of the HIGH SPEED push button on the throttle levers. Use of the HIGH SPEED button is permissible, but a rapid change in thrust will be effected.

2-30. BEFORE TAKE-OFF.

Pilots

a. Airplane in position for take-off. Brakes set.

b. Throttles retarded just below taxi thrust.

Engineer

a. Fuel Selector Valves - Check "TANK TO ENGINE AND MANIFOLD.

b. Fuel Pumps - "ON" in all Bomb Bay Tanks and Main Tanks. "OFF" in Auxiliary Tanks.

c. Trim Flaps - Nose-up trim, as necessary. Approximately 0 to 3° nose-up with CG of 25-26%.

d. Wing Slot Door Switch - "OPEN." This is a precautionary measure. The doors are automatically held open when the weight of the airplane is on the gears.

NOTE

Rudder trim is always neutral when the gear is down.

e. Landing Flaps - Check indicator flaps up.

f. When ready for T.O. advance all throttles to full open, using the HIGH SPEED advance, then move the emergency throttle disengage levers to the manual position.

NOTE

The reason for T.O. with manual throttle control is to permit the throttles to be "chopped" more quickly if it should be necessary.

g. Notify engineer to check instruments.

c. Fuel Shut-Off Valves - "OPEN" for Bomb Bay Tanks and Main Tank supply. "CLOSED" for Auxiliary Tanks.

"Run 'er Up Against the Brakes For T.O."

g. Check all instruments and if readings are normal, notify the pilot, "OK for take-off."

2-31. TAKE-OFF.

2-32. T.O. CHARACTERISTICS.- The airplane will fly off with gentle back-pressure on the control column; the airspeed depending on the gross weight of the airplane. As the airplane leaves the ground there is an apparent excessive nose-high attitude. This is a peculiarity of this type aircraft and should not cause alarm.

Do Not Be Alarmed at the Nose-High Attitude on Take-Off

2-33. DIRECTIONAL CONTROL DURING T.O.- On the take-off run, directional control is maintained first with the steerable nose wheel and then the rudders as speed increases.

2-34. NORMAL TAKE-OFF PROCEDURE.

2-35. After the engineer has given the O.K. for T.O., the pilot will release the brakes and take over the nose-wheel steering handle and hold the nose wheel on the ground with full forward pressure on the control column. Do not use the brakes except in an emergency. The copilot should call airspeeds to the pilot so that he may devote all of his attention to the runway.

WARNING

Do not use the rudder pedals while the trigger switch on the steering handle or control column is held. The brakes will be applied violently if the pedals are operated while either of these switches is actuated.

"Don't Use Rudder Pedals to Brake Wheels on T.O."

At 75-85 mph the rudders will become effective. The pilot can then release the steering handle and return the column to about neutral. At around 100 mph, raise the nose wheel and at about 115 mph lift the airplane off the ground.

2-36. As soon as the airplane is airborne, brake the wheels by pulling out on the parking brake control handle momentarily, then signal the copilot to raise the gear.

WARNING

> The reason for using the parking brake and not the normal foot brakes is that applying the foot brakes will also operate the rudders which is undesirable on take-off. Be sure to release the parking brake handle.

NOTE

> The airspeed should be held to less than 175 mph until gear is up and doors locked. Approximately one-minute is required for full retraction of the gears.

2-37. For adequate engine compartment cooling, high engine powers and low airspeeds, in the region of 125 to 175 mph should be avoided. (See paragraph 1-79.) During the run and take-off the airplane will be operating in this region so the gear should be retracted as soon as possible. This will permit the airspeed to be increased normally as soon as a safe altitude has been reached.

2-38. As soon as a safe altitude and airspeed have been reached and all obstacles cleared, retard the throttles to climb rpm. Move the emergency throttle disengage levers to the automatic position. Have the engineer re-engage his throttle levers with the motor-drive units by holding each TRIM switch in turn so as to retard each motor unit to the throttle lever position and engaging the notch in the motor-drive bellcrank by lifting one of the "triggers" and then allowing them to move full down into the notch. Place the wing slot doors control switch in the "AUTO" position. (Reference paragraph 2-50.)

2-39. MINIMUM RUN TAKE-OFF.- Same as normal take-off.

2-40. ENGINE FAILURE DURING TAKE-OFF. (See Section III, paragraph 3-17.)

2-41. CLIMB.

2-42. Place the FUEL SELECTOR VALVES on "TANK TO ENGINE."

2-43. Refer to the "Take-off, Climb, and Landing Chart" in Appendix I.

2-44. NORMAL CLIMB.- An airspeed of about 300 mph is best suited for a normal climb. During the climb the Flight Engineer may use the throttle TRIM switches to make minor throttle changes to balance engine rpms.

2-45. OBSTACLE CLIMB.- Clearing obstacles on the climb-out after take-off should be made with an airspeed of at least 20 mph above the take-off speed to avoid control difficulties.

2-46. NORMAL FLIGHT.

2-47. See the Flight Operation Instruction Charts in Appendix I. Use pitot and control bellows heat if necessary. Regulate cabin temperature, pressurization, or ventilation as desired.

SAD PLIGHT OF THE PILOT WHO INSISTED ON FLYING AT LOW ALTITUDE...

"It'll Go Farther At High Altitude"

2-48. FLIGHT CONTROL SURFACES.

2-49. CONTROL AT LOW IAS.- The hydraulic power boost systems are designed to operate at a minimum of 50% rpm engine speed for most satisfactory operation of the flight surfaces. At low IAS lateral and longitudinal control is adequate, but directional control may be difficult. To correct for yaw at low speed open both rudders momentarily.

2-50. CHARACTERISTICS OF WING SLOT DOORS.- As the wing slot doors close, the airplane will nose down abruptly and then will return to the original trim conditions.

2-51. THROTTLE OPERATION.

2-52. GENERAL.- **At altitudes above 10,000** feet move the throttles normally. Do not use the HIGH SPEED push-button control. The engineer may make minor throttle changes to synchronize engine rpms with the throttle TRIM switches. If the trim range is not sufficient, disengage the throttle and operate it manually. When this is done, the pilot cannot control that engine. See Section III for emergency operation of the throttles.

"Don't Use High Speed Retard Above 10,000 Ft."

2-53. STALLS.

2-54. STALL SPEEDS.- Stall speeds vary depending on the gross weight and CG of the airplane. A stall with a rearward center of gravity is more violent with a tendency for the airplane to drop off into a spin. An airspeed of at least 20 mph above the stall speed should be maintained at all times.

TABULATED STALL SPEEDS

Gross Weight	Take-Off (Flaps Up)	Landing (Flaps Down)	Clean
100,000	85	82	85
160,000	108	104	108
210,000	125	120	125

2-55. STALL WARNING.- **No stall warning is** felt in the form of control force reversal. This is due to the fact that the elevons are power operated. A stall may be defined as that point where there is an uncontrolled sharp drop of the nose or a rapid drop of one wing. It should be remembered that as the wing slot doors close, the nose will drop suddenly, which in this case would not indicate a stall.

2-56. STALL RECOVERY.- **Recovery from a stall is made by dropping the nose and using rudder and elevon control to prevent roll.**

2-57. SPINS.

2-58. GENERAL.- **Intentional spins are prohibited in this airplane. There is no tendency for the airplane to spin inadvertently in either the cruising or landing attitude. A roll from a stall may develop into a spin particularly with a rearward center of gravity.**

2-59. SPIN CHARACTERISTICS.- Although spin test data has not been compiled, wind tunnel tests indicate that a spin would be very steep with some oscillation, losing about 1800 feet per turn.

2-60. SPIN RECOVERY.- Wind tunnel tests show that recovery from a spin may be effected in approximately 2-1/2 turns by moving the control column forward and reversing the wheel, leaving the rudder with the spin. The tests indicated that rudder reversal retarded recovery.

2-61. DIVING.

2-62. **The pilot's airspeed indicator is equipped with a mach indicator which shows the maximum permissible airspeed at any altitude. Abrupt pull-outs at high speeds should be avoided.**

2-63. APPROACH AND LANDING.

2-64. The following check must be made during the approach:

Pilots	Engineer
a. Landing Gross Weight and C.G. - Check.	a. Electric System - Check.
b. Command Radio - "ON."	b. Hydraulic Pressures - Check.
c. Rudder Trim and Wing Slot Doors- Neutral and "OPEN."	c. Fuel Selector Valves - On "TANK TO ENGINE AND MANIFOLD."
d. Landing Gear - Down. Airspeed not to exceed 175 mph.	
e. Landing Flaps - Down. Airspeed not to exceed 160 mph.	

Pilots

f. Trim Flaps - Nose-up as necessary.

g. Throttle Disengage Levers - Down to manual position just before "touch down" or immediately after.

Engineer

2-65. NORMAL LANDING. (See figure 2-3.)- The landing flaps on this airplane lower the stall speed only slightly, but they appreciably steepen the glide path of the airplane. If, during the approach, it becomes desirable to reduce the airspeed, the rudders may be opened simultaneously. This procedure should not be used under 200 feet until pilots are familiar with the characteristics of the airplane. Although rudder trim will automatically be returned to neutral when the gear is lowered, as a safety measure it is suggested that the rudder trim be placed in neutral before lowering the gear for landing. In general, lower the gear at 175 mph, lower the landing flaps at 160 mph, use a nose-up trim as necessary, and reduce the airspeed until 115-125 mph is indicated "over the fence."

"Don't Lower Flaps Above 160 Mph."

CAUTION

If for any reason the trim flaps should fail, land with the landing flaps up. This is because the trim flaps are used to trim out the negative pitch moment caused by the lowering of the landing flap. If the trim flaps are inoperative and the landing flaps down it would be very difficult to control the airplane for a proper landing flare.

As soon as the airplane is on the ground, hold the nose wheel down and use the steerable nose wheel for directional control. To reduce the landing roll, the six inboard engines may be cut to reduce thrust. The brakes may be applied by using the rudder pedals, or the parking brake handle may be pulled out to apply the brakes evenly. Do not raise the landing flaps until the speed has dropped below 50 mph. See the "Take-Off, Climb, and Landing Chart" in Appendix I.

2-66. TAKE-OFF IF LANDING IS NOT COMPLETED.- Advance the throttles and retrim the airplane. Raise the landing flaps and gear when the airplane is clear of the ground and then assume a normal climbing angle maintaining less than 175 mph until the gears are up and the doors are closed.

2-67. STOPPING THE ENGINES.

Pilots	Engineer
a. Flight Controls - Move all surfaces to neutral, landing flaps up.	a. Throttles - Disengage each throttle lever in turn and manually move it rapidly to the "CLOSED" position.
b. Gyros - "CAGED."	b. Fuel Pumps - "OFF."
	c. Fuel Tank Shut-Off Valves - "CLOSED."

2-68. BEFORE LEAVING THE AIRPLANE.

Pilots	Engineer
a. Parking Brakes - Set. CAUTION Do not set parking brakes if they are hot.	a. Motor-Generator Switches - "OFF."
b. Radios - "OFF."	b. Ring Bus Relays - "OFF."

Pilots

c. Lights - "OFF."

d. See that the wheels are chocked.

e. Parking Brakes - Off.

f. Report malfunctions to Crew Chief.

Engineer

c. Load Off Switches - Trip Momentarily.

d. A.P.U. Relay Switches - "OFF."

e. Exciter Switches - "OFF."

f. Stop A.P.U.'s by operating them at idle speed for 30 seconds then cutting the ignition switches.

g. Battery Switch - "OFF."

h. Control Switches - Turn "OFF."

i. Report any malfunctions to the Crew Chief.

PILOTS NOTES

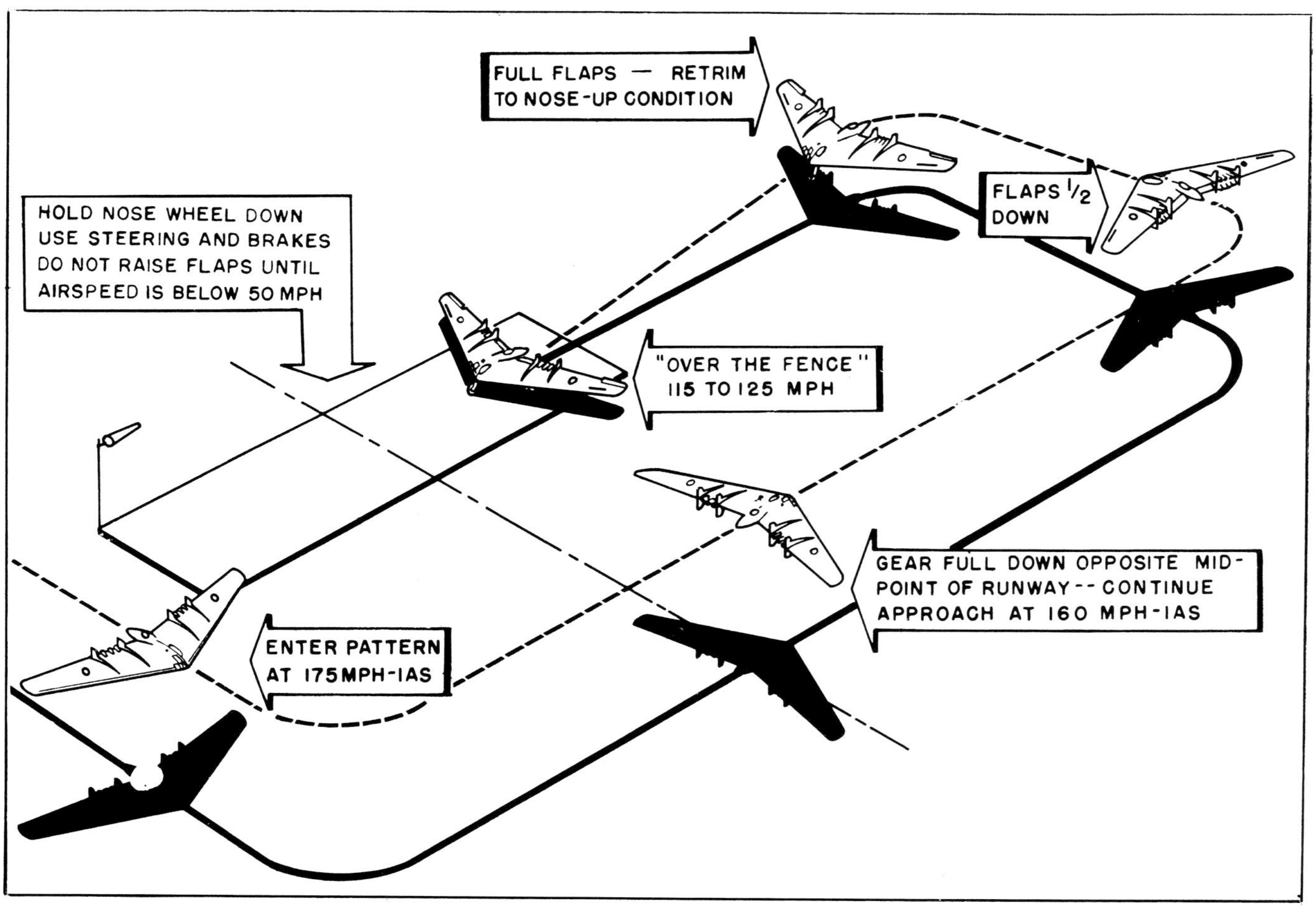

Figure 2-3. Traffic Pattern

SECTION III

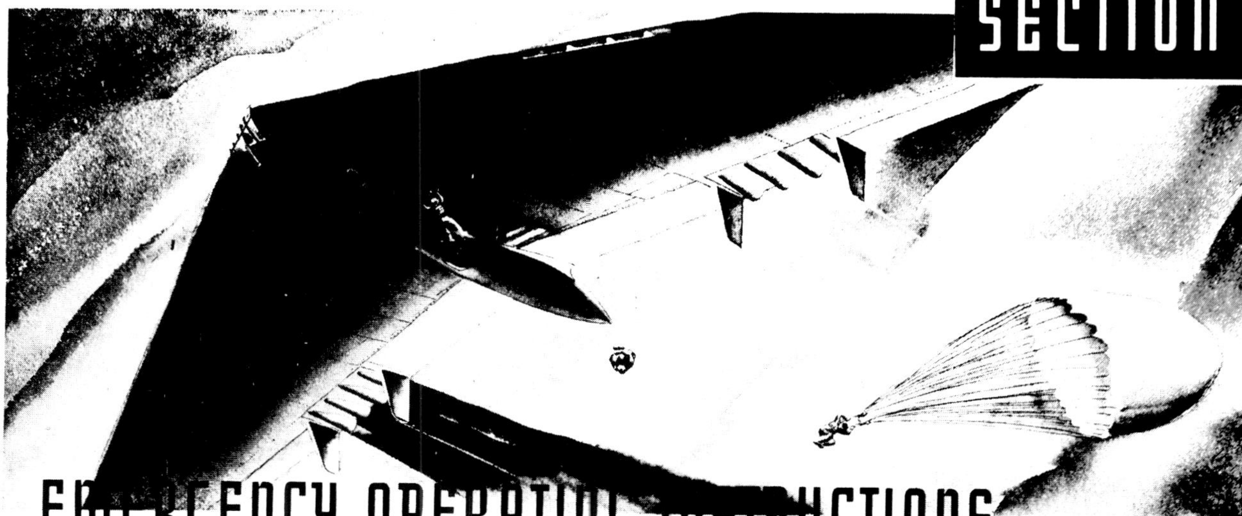

EMERGENCY OPERATING INSTRUCTIONS

3-1. EMERGENCY ESCAPE.

3-2. GENERAL.

3-3. All escape hatches are plainly stencilled. (See figure 3-1.) Before opening the escape hatch leading into No. 4 bomb bay, the bomb bay door must be opened. The door can be opened from the bombardier's station, pilot's station, or by a switch at each side of the escape hatch. The pilots' control will open all bomb bays and salvo all bombs safe. (See figure 3-2.) The switch located at the forward side of the escape hatch will open No. 4 bomb bay door and salvo bombs in that bay. The switch at the aft side of the

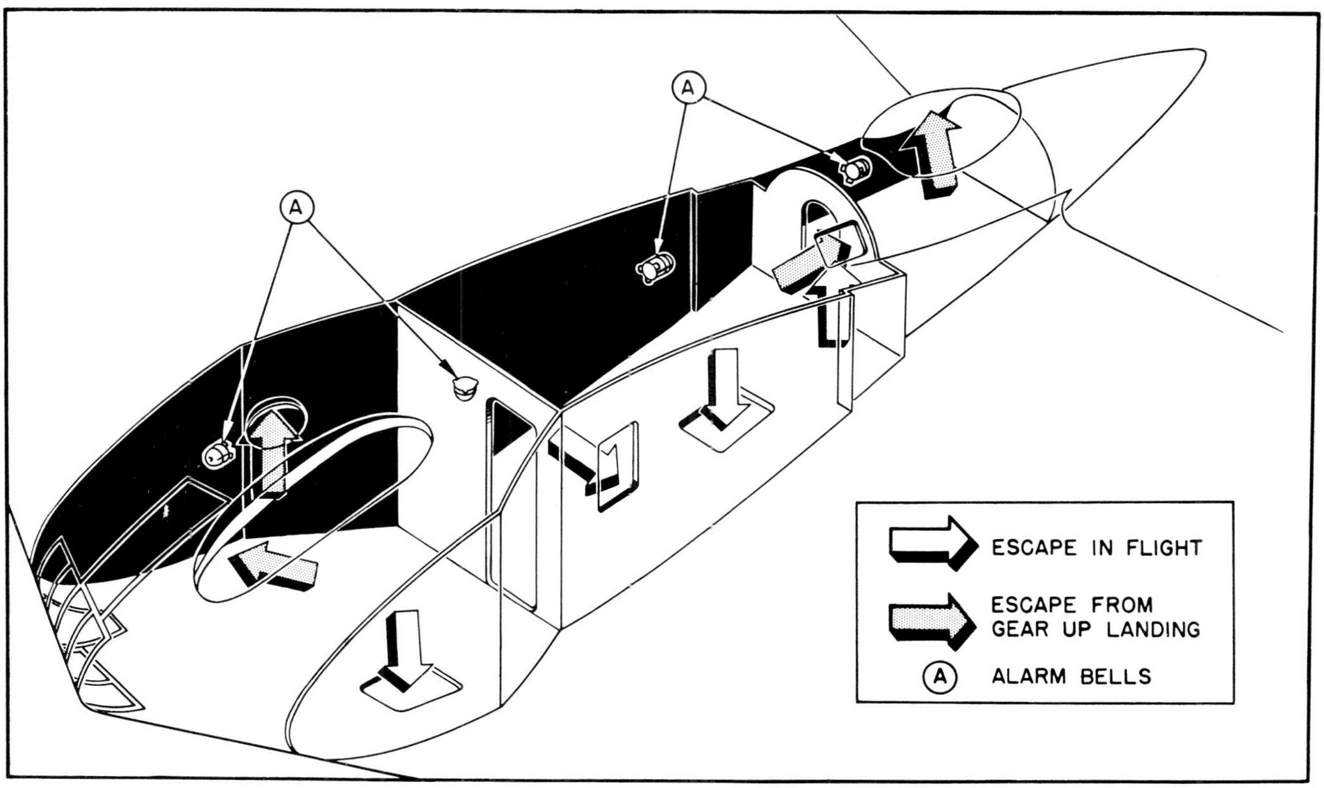

Figure 3-1. Escape Hatches

Figure 3-2. Pilot's Bomb Salvo Switch (On Wall To Left of Pilot)

hatch will open all bomb bay doors and salvo all bombs. (See figure 3-3.) If this hatch is to be used for escape, one of the bomb

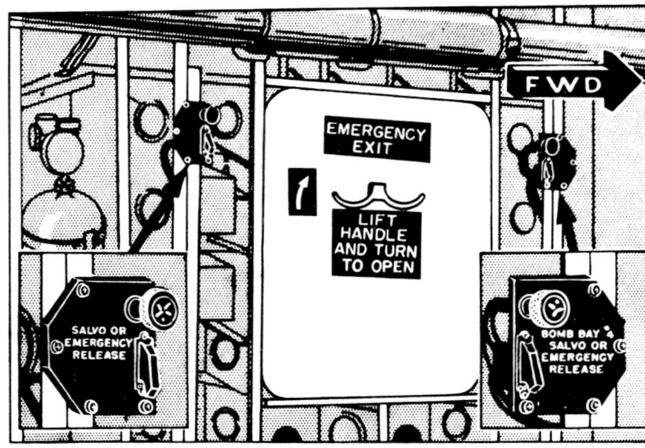

Figure 3-3. Bomb Bay #4 Opening and Salvo Switches

bay door switches should be tripped and a minimum of 10 seconds allowed before opening the escape hatch. The reason for this is that the hatch opens outward and, should the bomb bay door be only partially open, the hatch could fall on the door causing it to jam.

3-4. ESCAPE IN FLIGHT.

Pilots	Crew Members
a. Give three short rings on the emergency alarm bell to alert the crew.	
b. Instruct the radio operator to contact ground stations.	b. Prepare for bailout.
c. Have the crew members open the main entrance hatch, bomb bay No. 4 door and escape hatch, and the forward escape hatch.	c. Radio Operator: Contact ground stations giving necessary information. Crew Members: Open hatches as directed.
d. If the airplane is carrying bombs, salvo them "safe" over an unpopulated area.	
e. Have the crew members take the first aid kits.	
f. Turn "ON" the emergency alarm bell (see 4 figure 1-30) and instruct crew to bail out.	f. Radio Operator: Give location and time of bailout.

3-5. EMERGENCY ESCAPE ON THE GROUND.-

If time and conditions do not permit the use of the astrodome and upper escape hatch for exit, use the crash axes to escape. See figure 3-4 for locations of axes.

3-6. FIRE.

3-7. ENGINE SECTION FIRE.- The heat detector lights, 1 figure 1-16, indicate overheating and a possible fire condition. If an amber light comes on, decrease the power on that engine. If a red light comes on shut the engine off and watch the fire detector lights. In the event of an engine fire proceed as follows:

Pilots	Engineer
	a. Notify pilot.
b. Alert the crew and have the necessary exits opened in case the airplane should have to be abandoned.	b. Disengage and close the throttle for the engine in the affected zone.

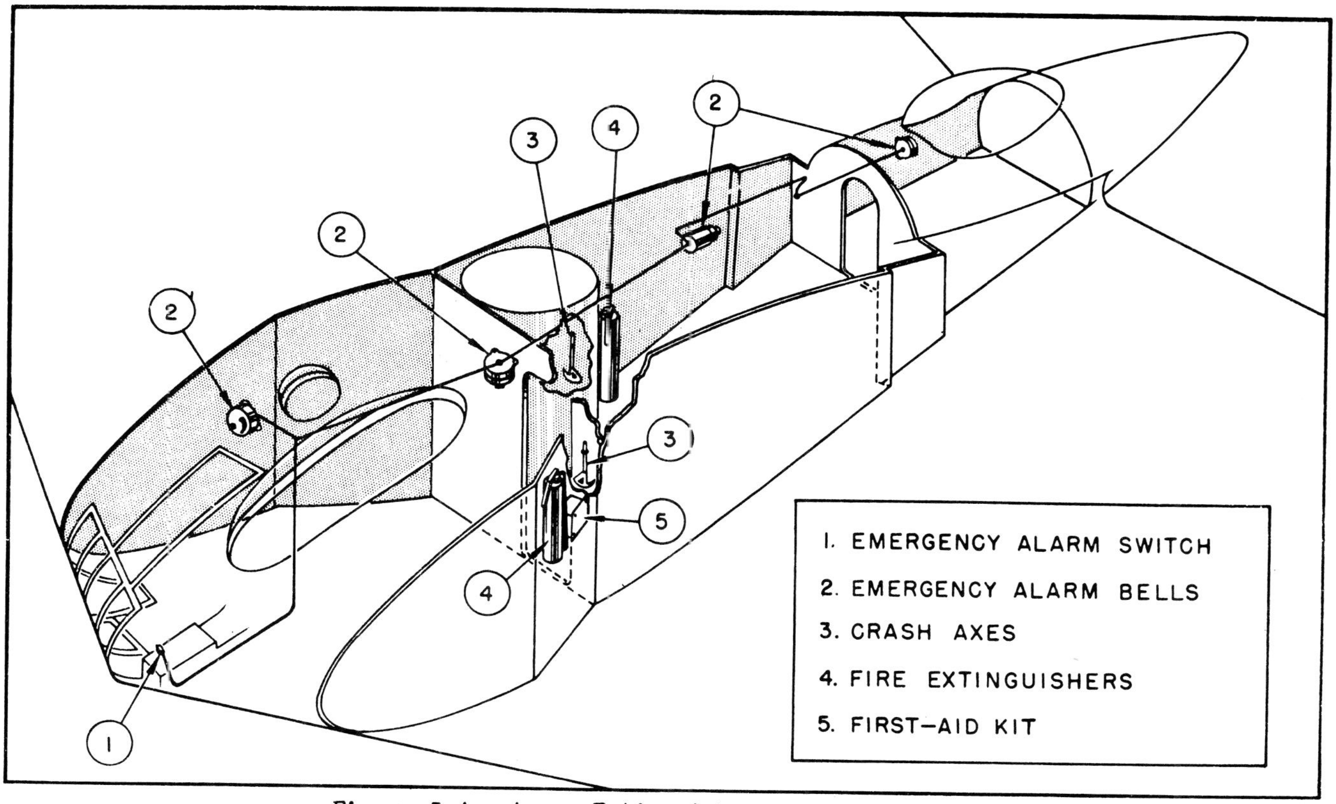

Figure 3-4. Axes, Extinguishers, and First Aid Kit

Pilots

c. Turn the CABIN AIR switch "OFF" for the affected side. (See figure 4-3.)

Engineer

c. Turn the fuel selector valve for the engine "OFF." (See figure 1-25.)

d. "CLOSE" the CABIN AIR SHUT-OFF BY-PASS VALVE switch.

e. Turn the fire extinguisher ZONE SELECTOR SWITCH to the burning zone.

f. Hold the appropriate discharge switch, up - first fire, down - second fire, for six seconds. After the fire is out, the indicator light will go out.

WARNING

If a third fire should occur in the same side, abandon the airplane.

g. Return the ZONE SELECTOR SWITCH to the "OFF" position.

h. Do not restart the engine or turn on the cabin air on the side in which the fire occurred.

3-8. A.P.U. FIRE.

Pilots

b. Alert the crew and open the escape hatches in case if should be necessary to abandon the airplane.

Engineer

a. Notify pilot.

b. Turn "OFF" the ignition for the affected A.P.U. and trip the LOAD OFF and the A.P.U. RELAY switches. (See figure 1-5.)

c. Turn the FUEL PUMP switch "OFF."

Pilots

Engineer

d. "CLOSE" A.P.U. Cooling Flap. (See 17 figure 1-12.)

e. Hold the discharge switch to the appropriate direction for six seconds. (See figure 1-39.)

f. Do not restart the affected unit.

g. Turn "ON" all RING BUS RELAY switches so that ac power from the one A.P.U. will be distributed throughout the airplane.

3-9. WING FIRE.- In the event of a wing fire beyond the reach of the engine section fire extinguisher system, attempt to put out the fire by yawing the airplane.

3-10. CREW NACELLE FIRE.- If a fire should occur in the nacelle, see that all hatches and the manual pressure regulator at the engineer's station are closed. "CLOSE" the CABIN AIR switch for the SHUT-OFF BY-PASS VALVE. Use a hand-operated fire extinguisher immediately.

3-11. ENGINE FUEL SYSTEM EMERGENCY OPERATION.

3-12. ENGINE FAILURE. (See figure 3-5.)

3-13. FUEL TANK FAILURE. (See figure 3-6.)

3-14. A.P.U. FUEL SYSTEM EMERGENCY OPERATION.

3-15. A.P.U. FAILURE.- If one A.P.U. should fail, turn the respective FUEL PUMP switch "OFF." This will stop the booster pump and close the fuel valve to that A.P.U.

3-16. A.P.U. FUEL BOOSTER PUMP FAILURE. (See figure 3-7.)- If a fuel booster pump should fail, turn its switch to "CROSS-FEED." Leave the other FUEL PUMP switch "ON."

3-17. ENGINE FAILURE.

3-18. If an engine should fail, turn its FUEL SELECTOR VALVE "OFF." Refer to figure 3-5 for operation of the fuel system.

3-19. ENGINE FAILURE BEFORE LEAVING THE GROUND ON TAKE-OFF.- In the event of an engine failure during the take-off run, don't take-off unless sufficient flying speed has been attained so that all obstacles can be cleared. Disengage the throttle for the affected engine and move it to the "CLOSED" position immediately. If flying speed has not been reached, or it is felt that obstacles cannot be cleared, apply maximum brakes without skidding the tires. It is possible to retract the landing gear by moving the EMERGENCY RELEASE lever to one side and then moving the landing gear control handle to the "UP" position. However, when this is done, the landing gear fairing doors must first open before the gear will move then the nose gear will retract sideways and in all probability the main gears will strike their fairing doors as they retract.

3-20. ENGINE FAILURE AFTER LEAVING THE GROUND ON TAKE-OFF.- Should an engine fail on the take-off, retract the landing gear, disengage the individual throttle and move it to the "CLOSED" position. Balance the eccentric thrust with the rudders momentarily, then allow the airplane to yaw up to 10° while reducing rudder deflection. This procedure will give minimum drag and allow the airplane to be more easily controlled. Level off to pick up airspeed and then continue climbing as deemed desirable.

3-21. ENGINE FAILURE DURING FLIGHT.- Follow the procedure in paragraph 3-20 as necessary. Trim the airplane as conditions require and increase the power on the remaining engines to maintain the desired airspeed.

3-22. RESTARTING ENGINES IN FLIGHT.

3-23. In the event of a blowout in flight an air start may be made in the following manner:

a. Pull the nose of the airplane up to drain the combustion chambers.

b. Be sure that the throttle for that engine is "CLOSED."

c. Turn the fuel selector valve to "TANK TO ENGINE" or in a position consistant with fuel usage.

d. The ignition on this airplane will permit air starts up to approximately 43,000 feet. Windmilling rpm for starting at altitude is approximately 35%.

e. Close the ignition switch and open the throttle slowly. The fuel pressure required for starting at altitude is much higher than that for ground starts.

f. Observe the tail pipe temperature indicator for firing of the engine and allow the engine to operate in a retarded condition until the tail pipe temperature stabilizes. Then advance the throttle slowly and engage it with the pilots' follow-up arm assembly and the motor-drive bellcrank.

g. If the starting attempt is unsuccessfull, close the throttle and repeat the starting procedure.

ENGINE FAILURE

DIAGRAM SHOWS #8 ENGINE OUT AND FUEL TO THAT ENGINE CUTOFF.

1. SELECTOR VALVE FOR AFFECTED ENGINE "OFF."
2. TURN "OFF" THE FUEL PUMPS FOR THAT ENGINE.
3. TRANSFER FUEL TO OTHER TANKS TO MANTAIN EVEN TANK LEVELS.

IF TWO ADJACENT ENGINES, SUCH AS #7 AND #8, SHOULD FAIL, THE SELECTOR VALVES FOR THESE TWO ENGINES MAY BE PLACED ON "TANK TO MANIF." THEN BY TURNING "OFF" THE #4 MAIN TANK SHUT-OFF VALVE AND LEAVING THE BOOSTER PUMPS OPERATING, FUEL WILL BE PUMPED INTO THE ENGINE MANIFOLD WHERE IT CAN BE TRANSFERRED INTO THE OTHER MAIN TANKS OR SUPPLIED TO THE OTHER ENGINES.

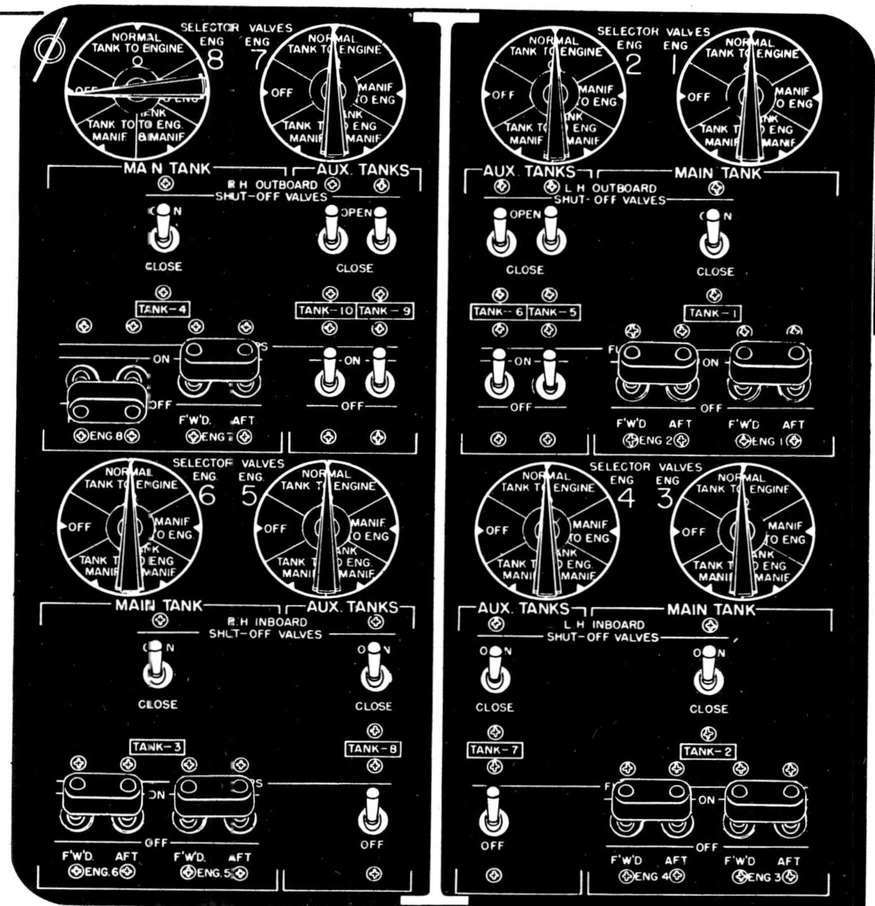

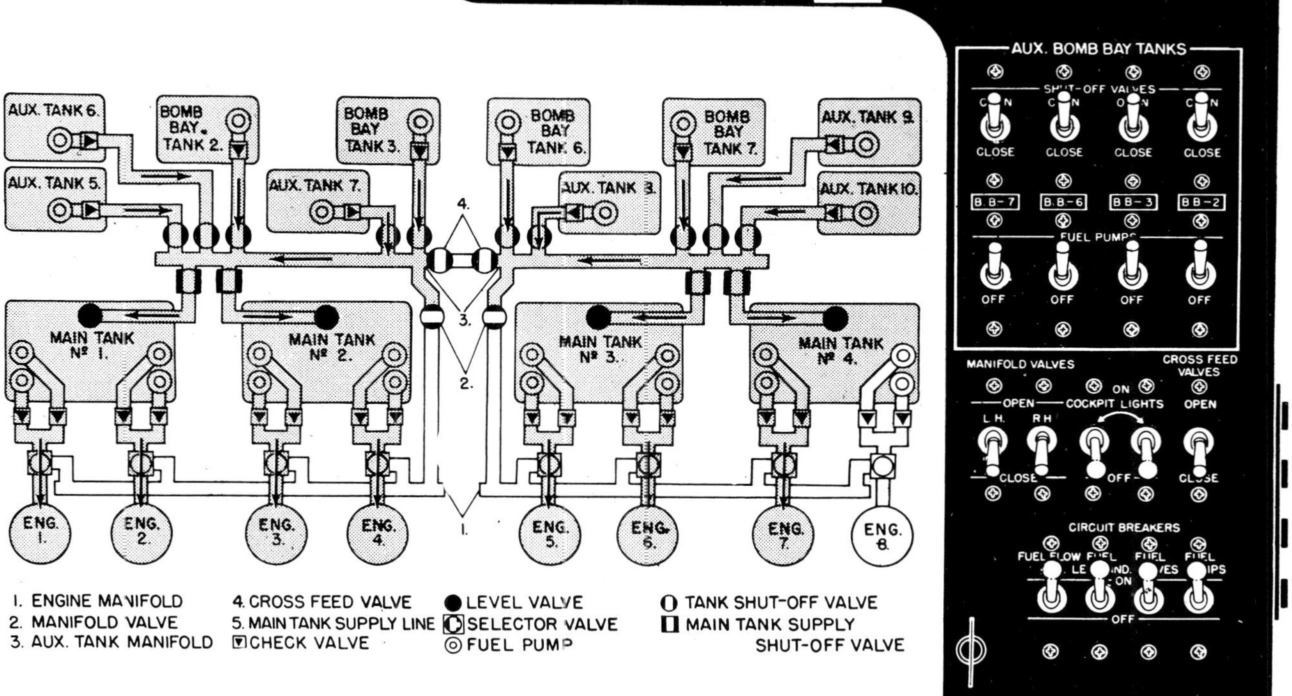

Figure 3-5. Fuel System Operation - Engine Failure

MAIN TANK AND AUX. TANK FAILURE

DIAGRAM SHOWS #1 MAIN TANK AND AUX. TANK #6 AS HAVING FAILED.

1. MAIN TANK FAILURE:
   a. SELECT "MANIF TO ENG." FOR BOTH ENGINES RECEIVING FUEL FROM THIS MAIN TANK.
   b. SELECT "TANK TO ENGINE AND MANIF." FOR THE OTHER TWO ENGINES CONNECTED TO THIS ENGINE MANIFOLD.
   c. CLOSE THE TANK VALVE AND TURN OFF THE FUEL PUMPS.
   d. FOR A SECOND MAIN TANK EMERGENCY FOLLOW STEPS a,b & c ABOVE THEN OPEN BOTH MANIFOLD VALVES AND THE CROSS-FEED VALVES.
2. AUXILIARY TANK FAILURE:
   a. CLOSE THE TANK VALVE.
   b. TURN OFF THE FUEL PUMP.

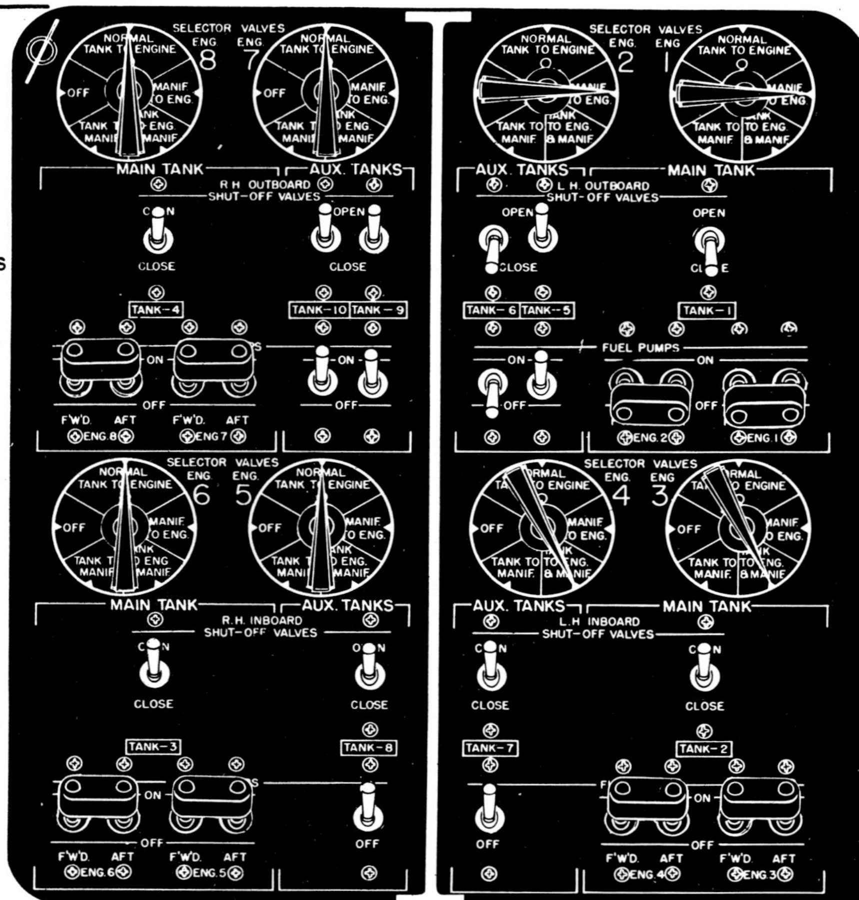

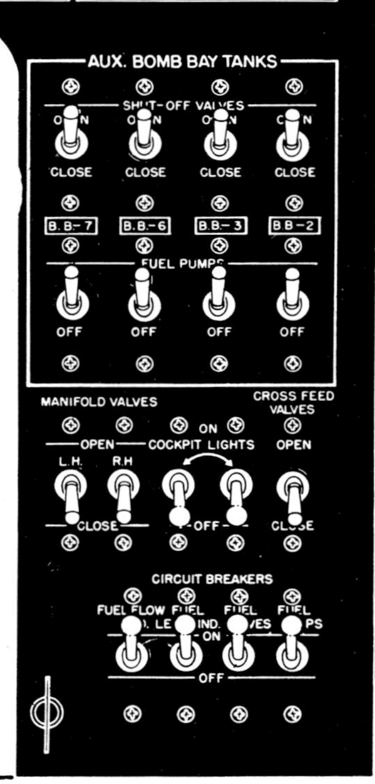

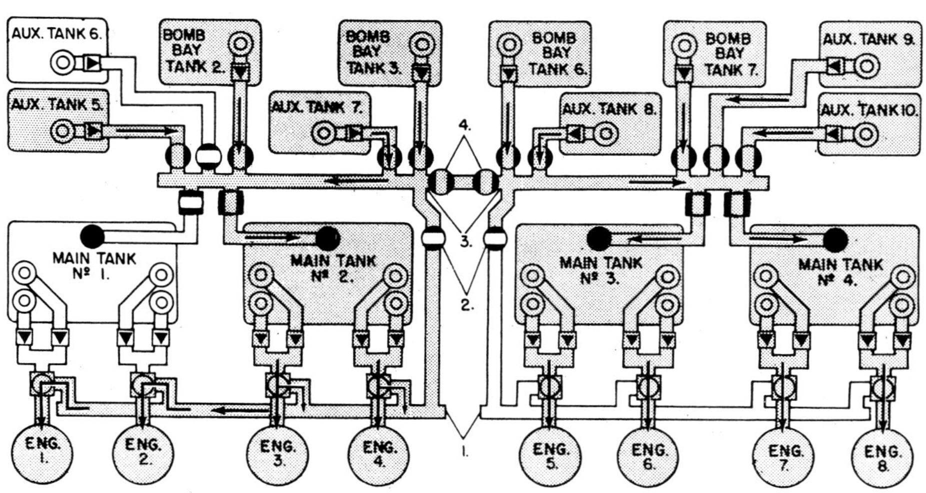

1. ENGINE MANIFOLD
2. MANIFOLD VALVE
3. AUX. TANK MANIFOLD
4. CROSS FEED VALVE
5. MAIN TANK SUPPLY LINE

● LEVEL VALVE
SELECTOR VALVE
CHECK VALVE
◎ FUEL PUMP
TANK SHUT-OFF VALVE
MAIN TANK SUPPLY SHUT-OFF VALVE

Figure 3-6. Fuel System Operation - Tank Failure

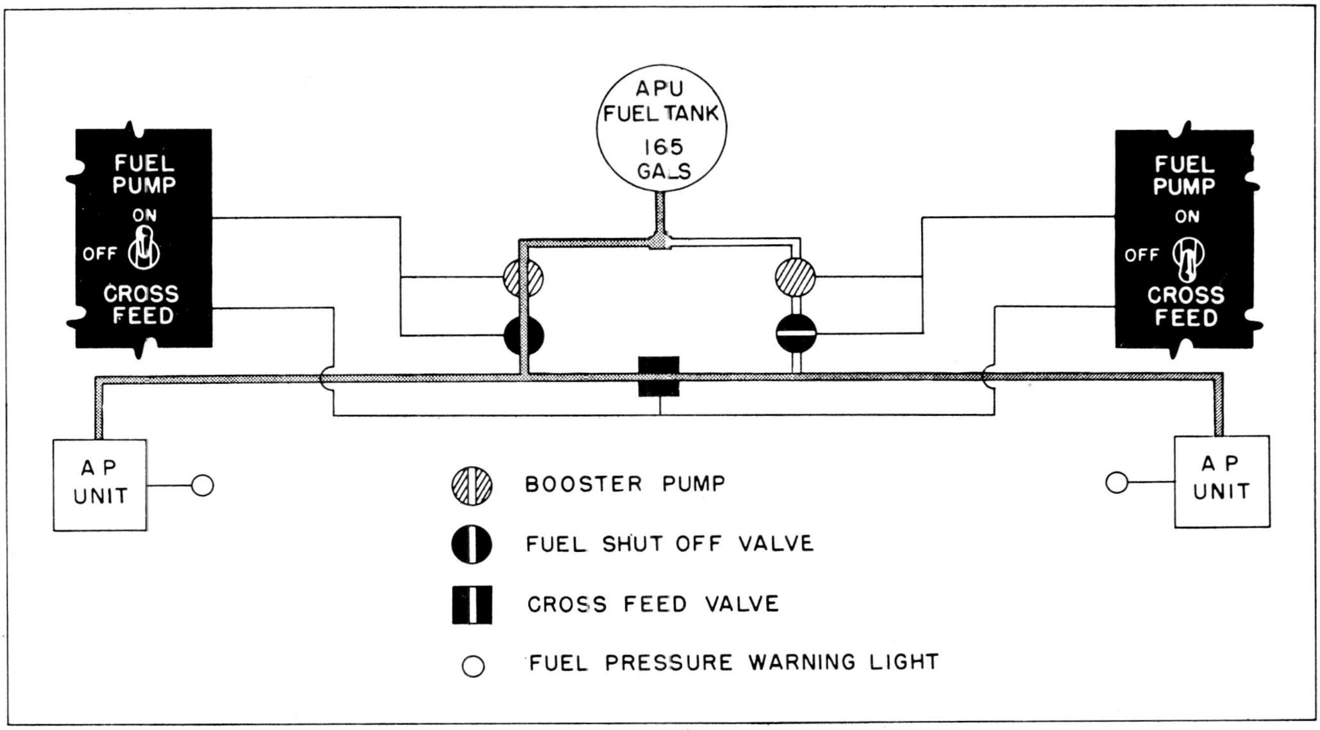

Figure 3-7. A.P.U. Fuel System Emergency Operation

3-24. FLIGHT-CONTROL SURFACE EMERGENCY OPERATION.

3-25. Only the elevons and landing flaps have provisions for emergency operation.

3-26. ELEVON EMERGENCY OPERATION.- If for any reason the elevons should fail to respond to normal control, engage the emergency electrical system by closing the switch on the pilot's control wheel and then turning "ON" the EMERGENCY ELEVON CONTROL switch located on the pilots' pedestal. (See figure 1-33 and 3 figure 1-30.) Control response will be the same as for the normal hydraulic control system. If the load limit lights come on, retrim the airplane to relieve the loads imposed on the system. If for any reason the control bellows should hold or bind on control column movement, release the disengage lever that is located at the forward side of the pilot's control column. (See figure 1-28.)

3-27. LANDING FLAP EMERGENCY OPERATION.

3-28. Failure of the landing flaps to operate can be from two causes: the flaps may have overrun their electrical limit switches in which case the mechanical stops have disengaged the motors from the gear box operating mechanism, or one flap motor may have failed.

3-29. ENGAGEMENT AFTER FLAP OVERRUN.- Note the direction of overrun and place the pilot's control switch in the opposite position. Reset the flap power unit by pulling the RESET handle (see figure 1-35) on the unit outboard as far as possible.

3-30. FAILURE OF ONE FLAP MOTOR.- If the flaps will not operate with the pilots' switch ON in the desired direction of travel turn "OFF" the MOTOR 1 selector switch and, if the flaps still do not operate, return this switch to the "ON" position and turn "OFF" the MOTOR 2 switch. (See figure 1-35.) Leave the switch for the inoperative motor in the "OFF" position. The selector switches are located on the flap power unit in the aft gunner's station.

3-31. AIR BRAKE EMERGENCY OPERATION.

3-32. When the landing gear is lowered using the emergency release system, the steering and brake pumps will not be started and likewise failure of the landing gear operated switch will prevent the operation of the steering and brake pumps. If the landing gear is lowered and the steering and brake system fails to operate, turn the HYD. BRAKE PUMP MANUAL OVERRIDE switch "ON." (See 16 figure 1-12.) If the system still fails to operate use the emergency air brakes to stop the airplane upon landing. Differential braking is possible by operating one handle more than the other, and even braking is accomplished by operating both handles together. (See figure 3-8.) Abrupt movement of the handles will result in violent braking action.

"Avoid Abrupt Operation"

Figure 3-8. Emergency Air Brake Control Levers (Between Pilots)

3-33. EMERGENCY LANDING-GEAR OPERATION.

3-34. Emergency lowering of the gear is possible but there are no provisions for emergency retraction while in flight if failure is due to an electrical fault. If the landing-gear handle down-safety solenoid should fail, mechanical provisions are made to release the handle so that the gear can be retracted.

3-35. EMERGENCY LOWERING OF THE GEAR.- In an emergency, instruct a member of the crew to operate the EMERGENCY LANDING-GEAR RELEASE handle that is located on the side of the crew nacelle turret structure. (See figure 1-37.) This handle operates in a manner similar to a ratchet wrench. A lever on the handle controls the direction of ratchet. A pointer assembly above the handle indicates the GEAR LOCKED or GEAR UNLOCKED condition. To lower the gear, first place the LANDING-GEAR CONTROL handle in the "DOWN" position, then move the lever on the EMERGENCY RELEASE handle to the UNLOCK position and raise the handle 90°, return the handle and repeat this 90° movement five times to unlock the gear. Be sure to turn "ON" the HYD. BRAKE PUMP MANUAL OVERRIDE switch to start the steering and brake system pumps.

CAUTION

Do not operate the emergency release above 140 mph.

3-36. EMERGENCY HANDLE RELEASE.- To retract the gear in the event the handle should be locked in the down position after take-off, move the EMERGENCY HANDLE RELEASE lever to one side (see figure 1-36) and then move the landing gear control handle to the "UP position.

3-37. LANDING WITH THE GEAR RETRACTED.

a. If the airplane is carrying bombs, drop them in a "safe" condition over an unpopulated area. Also, if feasible, circle the landing area to use up excessive fuel.

b. Prepare the crew for a crash landing.

c. Release all oxygen by turning the regulators to the extreme clock-wise position.

d. Have the astrodome and the upper escape hatch opened. If unable to remove astrodome use the ax.

e. Hold power on until the airplane has reached landing attitude just above stalling speed with the flaps down.

f. Have the engineer stop the A.P.U.'s.

g. Alert the crew at the moment preceding the "touch-down," and close the throttles.

h. After the airplane has come to rest, leave it immediately. Make sure that all crew members are out then move to a safe distance from the airplane.

3-38. LANDING IN WATER (DITCHING).

3-39. Ditching characteristics of this type airplane have not been definitely established. Tests with scale models, however, have given the following indications of what may be expected in making a water landing: The best attitude for contact seems to be at a normal landing attitude with the landing gear up and the flaps down and at the lowest possible forward speed. Upon contact, especially if one wing is low, the model indicates a tendency to yaw, and near the end of the run a moderate turn may develop. Neither the yaw nor turn appears to be dangerous, but personnel should be braced to withstand both lateral and longitudinal deceleration.

3-40. ELECTRICAL SYSTEM FAILURE.

3-41. CIRCUIT BREAKERS AND LIMITERS. See figure 1-3 for locations of limiters accessible in flight.

"Be Careful When Changing Limiters in Flight"

3-42. A.P.U. FAILURE. (Partial and complete ac failure.)

a. If one A.P.U. should fail, immediately hit the LOAD OFF switch and turn "OFF" the A.P.U. RELAY switch for the affected A.P.U. so as to cut this unit out of the ac system. Then turn "ON" ALL RING BUS RELAYS so that the remaining A.P.U. will supply power to all ac equipment. If an attempt is made to restart the A.P.U., be sure to turn "OFF" the BUS TIE RELAYS B and D.

b. If both A.P.U.'s should fail, a complete ac and dc power failure will occur. In this event the pilot should immediately engage the EMERGENCY ELEVON CONTROL switch and the engineer should turn "OFF" both motor-generators and then turn "ON" the starter-generators. The starter-generators will supply dc power for the operation of all dc equipment and also provide sufficient power for restarting the A.P.U.'s. With an ac failure the landing gear will have to be lowered by means of the emergency release system and the air brakes used to stop the airplane. Both the landing and trim flaps will be inoperative so a faster landing with a longer approach must be made.

3-43. MOTOR-GENERATOR FAILURE. (See paragraph 3-42b.)

3-44. If one motor-generator should fail, turn "OFF" the respective switch. See that the remaining generator is operating at 28v and 200 amperes. If desired, both motor-generators may be turned "OFF" and the starter-generators turned "ON" for dc power.

3-45. THROTTLE SYSTEM FAILURE.

3-46. THROTTLE DISENGAGEMENT.- If for any reason the throttle system fails to respond to normal operation, the pilot should move the "EMER. DISENGAGE" levers to the disengaged position. When this is done, the throttles will be controlled manually. Be sure to advance and retard the throttles slowly when on manual control, to prevent overheating the tail pipes or blowing out the fires. Make every effort to locate the cause of failure and correct it if possible.

3-47. THROTTLE RE-ENGAGEMENT.- Re-engage the normal throttle system in the following manner:

a. Move all throttles to the 96% rpm position.

b. Have the engineer hold his master throttle switch in the "ADVANCE" position until the throttle-drive-motors stop.

c. Move the pilot's "EMER. DISENGAGE" lever to the normal position.

d. By holding each throttle trim switch in turn to the "RETARD" position while holding up on one "trigger" and down on the other on the respective throttle the engineer can engage the motor-drive-units with the throttle levers.

3-48. EMERGENCY BOMB SALVO.

3-49. Bombs may be released in salvo from three positions in the airplane; from the bombardier's control panel, by a switch located to the left of the pilot or by a switch at the aft side of the No. 4 bomb bay escape hatch. The pilot's switch and the switch at the aft side of the escape hatch will salvo all bombs safe. The switch at the forward side of the escape hatch will salvo only the bombs in No. 4 bomb bay. When any salvo switch is operated, an indicator light on the bombardier's panel and the one next to the other salvo switches will light.

3-50. CREW NACELLE HEATING AND PRESSURIZATION EMERGENCY OPERATION.

3-51. CABIN PRESSURE EMERGENCY REGULATION OR AIR DUMP.- If the automatic pressure regulator or cabin air relief valve fails, causing the nacelle pressure to increase, the engineer's manual pressure regulator may be opened to regulate the pressure, or the emergency cabin air dump valve at the pilot's station may be operated. (See figure 4-3.) The pilot's cabin air dump will relieve the nacelle pressure, shut-off the pressurizing system, and extend the ram air scoop providing air for ventilation. Either one, but not both, of the cabin air valves may then be re-opened to provide heated air, if desired. No pressurization is possible, however, when the dump valve is open.

3-52. FAILURE OF HEATING AND PRESSURIZING SYSTEM.- If the system on one side of the airplane becomes inoperative, "CLOSE" the corresponding CABIN AIR VALVE switch, and the remaining system, controlled by its rheostat, will serve adequately. If both sides fail move both CABIN AIR VALVE switches to the "CLOSE" position. In this case the ram air scoop will automatically extend to supply ventilating air.

3-53. ALTITUDE WARNING HORNS.- At any time that the nacelle pressure drops below a 5000 foot pressure, two horns in the nacelle will blow. The horns may be turned off by means of a switch-type circuit breaker on the engineer's upper electrical panel. (See figure 1-10.)

3-54. FIGURE REFERENCES.

Emergency Escape ------------ figure 3-1
Bomb Salvo Switches---------- figures 3-2 and 3-3
Emergency Alarm Bell Switch -------------------- 4 figure 1-30
Crash Axes, Fire Extinguishers and First Aid Kit ---------------------- figure 3-4
Engine Fuel System Emergency Operation ----------- figures 3-5 and 3-6
A.P.U. Fuel System Emergency Operation ----------- figure 3-7
Emergency Elevon Control Switch -------------------- 3 figure 1-30
Landing Flap Emergency Controls ------------------ figure 1-35
Emergency Air Brake Controls ------------------ figure 3-8
Landing Gear Control Handle Release Lever ------ figure 1-36
Landing Gear Emergency Release Control Handle -------------------- figure 1-37
Throttle Emergency Disengage Levers ------------- figure 1-24
Cabin Air Emergency Dump Controls ------------- figure 4-3

PILOTS NOTES

SECTION IV

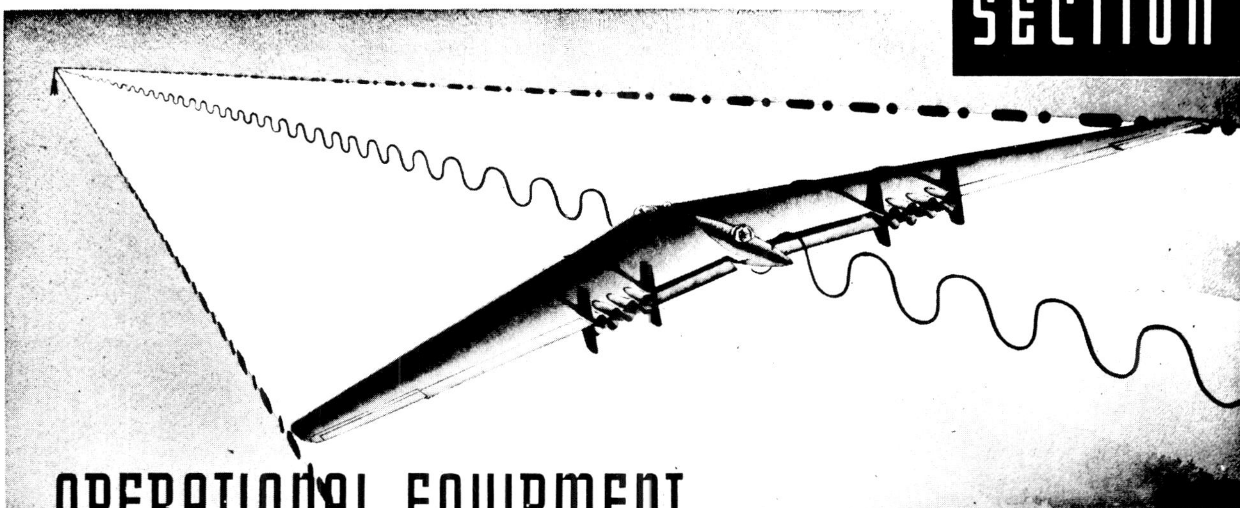

OPERATIONAL EQUIPMENT

4-1. OXYGEN.

4-2. GENERAL.

4-3. The airplane is equipped with a low pressure, demand type oxygen system, operating at a maximum working pressure of 425 psi. Oxygen equipment is furnished for a crew of 13. (See figure 4-1.) The crew is supplied with oxygen from 16 type G-1 cylinders. In addition to the normal system, there are four portable oxygen bottles and six hose assemblies for recharging the portable bottles.

4-4. USE OF OXYGEN. (See figure 4-2.)- Use oxygen above 10,000 feet, and at night use oxygen from the ground up with an unpressurized crew nacelle. Above 10,000 feet, use the portable bottles when moving about the airplane.

4-5. WING ANTI-ICING.- There are no provisions for wing anti-icing.

4-6. CREW NACELLE HEAT, VENT, AND PRESSURIZATION.

4-7. GENERAL.

4-8. The complete crew nacelle can be heated and pressurized. Hot air for heating, ventilating, defrosting, and pressurizing purposes is derived from the compressor section of the engines, a separate system on each side of the airplane. The air from each system is ducted through a shut-off valve and an after-cooler before entering the crew nacelle to be distributed to various crew stations. Each after-cooler incorporates a turbine, driven by the compressed air from the engines, which draws air from the respective bomb bay through the after-cooler for regulation of the cabin air temperatures. The cooling air is exhausted through a opening in each upper wing surface. The temperature of the air entering the crew nacelle is electrically regulated by the manual setting of two rheostat regulators in the crew nacelle. The regulators maintain or change the cabin air temperature as selected by the automatic positioning of flaps which regulate the flow of cooling air through the after-coolers. Crew nacelle pressure is controlled by an automatic pressure regulator installed aft of the turret structure in the crew's quarters. An emergency air dump and pressure relief valve is located at the pilot's station (see paragraph 3-50). A ram air duct is installed in bomb bay number four for use if the pressurized heating system becomes inoperative and also to supply ventilating air. (See figure 4-3.) Heating or cooling while on the ground is possible by extending the ram air duct and inserting a hose from a suitable air source. Four electric fans are provided in the crew nacelle for circulating the air.

4-9. HEATING AND VENTILATING CONTROLS.

4-10. CABIN AIR VALVE SWITCHES. (See figure 4-3.)- There are two CABIN AIR VALVE switches marked "LH" and "RH" at the pilot's station on the left crew nacelle wall. These switches operate the motor-drive for lowering the ram air scoop and the cabin air shut-off valve. When both switches are in the "CLOSED" position, the ram air duct is automatically extended. No heating or pressurizing of the air is accomplished by this intake.

4-11. TEMPERATURE REGULATING RHEOSTATS. (See figure 4-3.)- One rheostat (controlling the left-hand system) is located at the engineer's right, and the other rheostat (controlling the right-hand system) at the forward right side of the center crew nacelle. A range of control from 40°F (4.4°C) to 80°F (26.7°C) is provided at each rheostat.

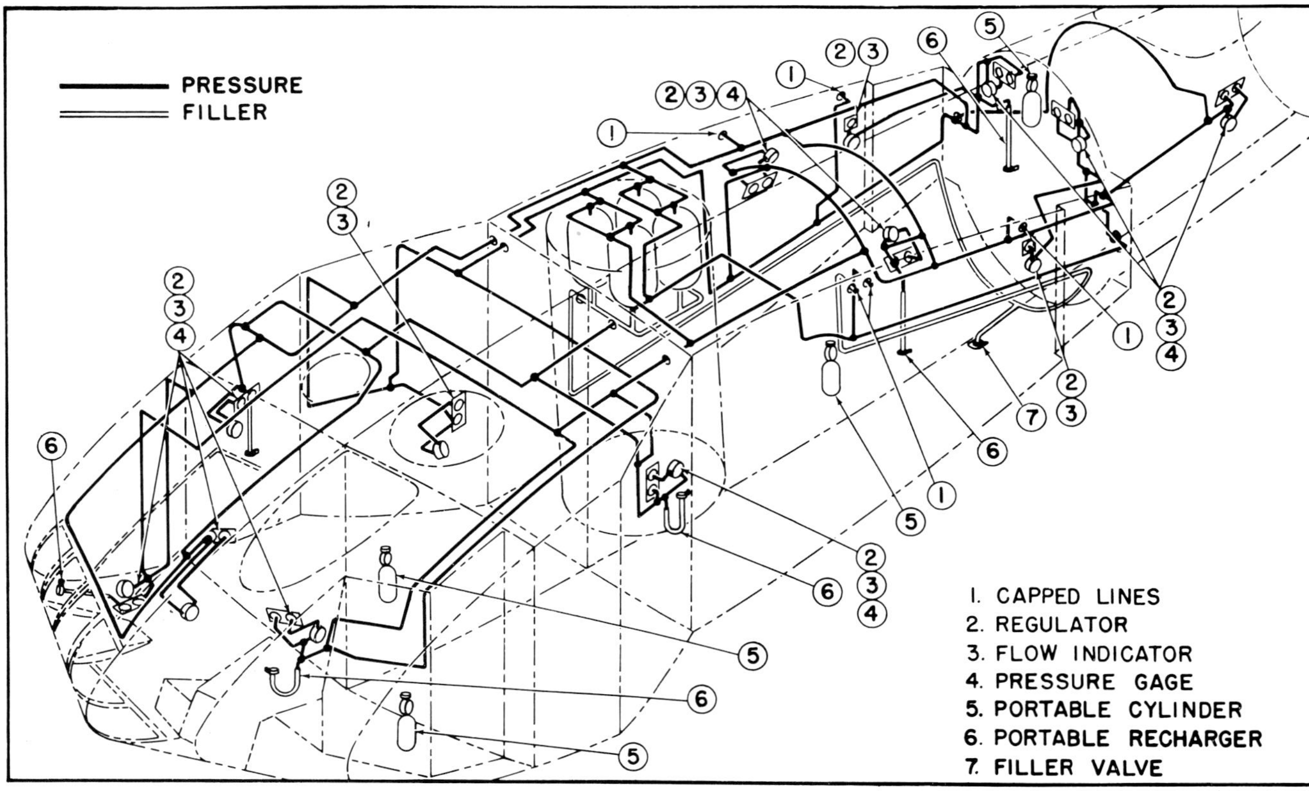

Figure 4-1. Oxygen System

4-12. SHUT-OFF BYPASS VALVE SWITCH. (See figure 4-3.)- This switch-type circuit breaker, mounted on the engineer's upper electrical panel, opens or closes a solenoid-operated bypass valve in a small line around the cabin air shut-off valve. The bypass is used to pre-rotate the after-cooler turbine so that when the cabin air is turned on, the sudden rush of air will not damage the turbine bearings. The normal position is "OPEN" at all times, except during fire extinguishing operation, when it must be closed.

4-13. CREW NACELLE PRESSURIZING CONTROLS.

4-14. AUTOMATIC PRESSURE REGULATOR.- The automatic pressure regulator is installed in the nacelle just aft of the center turret structure. This regulator is set to automatically maintain a 5,000-foot nacelle pressure up to approximately 28,500 feet altitude. Above that it maintains a differential air pressure of 7.45 psi between nacelle and atmospheric air pressure. There are no manual controls for the regulator.

4-15. MANUAL PRESSURE REGULATOR VALVE.- This valve is installed overhead at the engineer's station. The engineer can adjust this valve by turning the knob one way or the other to maintain proper nacelle pressure in the event that the automatic regulator should fail.

4-16. CABIN PRESSURE RELIEF AND EMERGENCY AIR DUMP VALVE.- This valve is installed in the nacelle wall to the pilot's left. The valve will automatically relieve the nacelle pressure at approximately 7.45 psi above atmospheric pressure. A switch-type lever permits the pilot to dump the cabin air for emergency depressurization.

4-17. OPERATION OF HEAT, VENT, AND PRESSURIZING SYSTEM.

CAUTION

The SHUT-OFF BYPASS VALVE switch must be "OPEN" before this system is turned on, to pre-rotate the heating system after-cooler turbine, preventing the sudden rush of high pressure air from causing bearing damage.

a. CABIN TEMP. CIRCUIT BREAKERS. (See figure 1-10.)- Have the engineer check the LH and RH circuit breakers on the upper electrical control to see that they are on.

b. CABIN AIR VALVE AND DUMP SWITCHES.- Move these switches down to "OPEN" for the shut-off valves and "CLOSE" the dump valve.

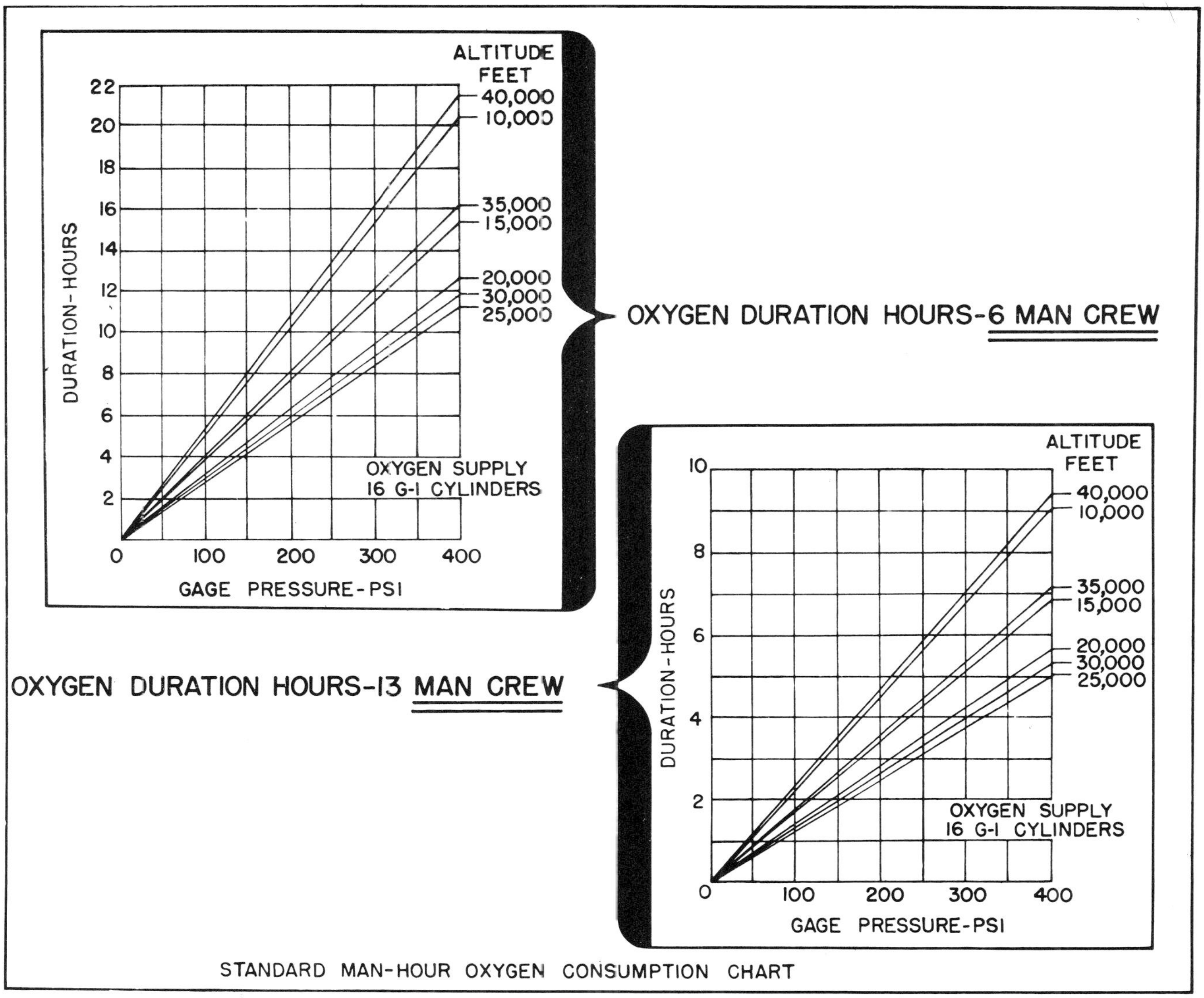

Figure 4-2. Standard Man-Hours Oxygen Consumption Charts

c. TEMPERATURE REGULATORS. Adjust for temperature desired.

WARNING

In case of a fire, "CLOSE" the CABIN AIR VALVE switch on the affected side, and move the SHUT-OFF BYPASS VALVE switch to the "CLOSE" position, until certain that all fire extinguisher agent has been discharged. For all other conditions of operation, the SHUT-OFF BYPASS VALVE switch must be "OPEN."

d. For heat and vent without pressurization, "CLOSE" the cabin air valves; this will automatically extend the ram air scoop. Then "OPEN" one cabin air valve, but not both, and adjust the respective temperature regulator for heat.

4-18. SUIT HEATER EQUIPMENT.

4-19. GENERAL.

4-20. Suit heater control boxes are located at each crew station. They operate on 30 volts ac and have plug-in receptacles and rheostat control knobs for voltage regulation.

4-21. RADIO EQUIPMENT.

4-22. TABLE OF COMMUNICATIONS AND RADIO EQUIPMENT.

TYPE	DESIGNATION	USE	OPERATOR	FREQ. RANGE	FIG. REF.
Interphone	AN/AIC-2	Inter airplane communication.	Press-to-talk buttons on each control wheel, foot switches for radio operator, bombardier, navigator, and engineer. Conventional hand switches for the remainder of the crew.	Audio frequencies.	
Radio Compass	AN/ARN-7	Reception of voice and code, navigation, and homing.	Pilot and navigator.	Complete coverage from 100KC to 1750KC.	Fig. 4-6, Item 4.
Low Frequency Range Receiver.	SCR-274	Low frequency range reception.	Pilots	Complete coverage from 190KC to 550KC.	4-7
Command.	AN/ARC-3	Voice and code communication within the 100 to 156 megacycle range.	Pilots	Any of eight pre-selected fixed frequencies between 100MC and 156MC.	Fig. 1-30, Item 12.
Liaison	AN/ARC-8	High frequency voice and code transmission and reception.	Radio operator.	<u>Receiver</u>: Complete coverage from 200KC to 500KC and 1.5MC to 18.0MC <u>Transmitter</u>: Complete coverage from 2.0MC to 18.1MC.	Fig. 4-4, Items 5 and 7.
Marker Beacon	RC-193	Navigation aid for identifying marker beacon signals.	Connected into the radio compass control circuit.	Fixed at 75MC.	
Identification	SCR-695	Automatic identification.	Pilot	<u>G-band</u>: Any one fixed position between 204MC and 211MC. <u>I-band</u>: Automatic sweep between 160MC and 185MC.	Fig. 4-5, Item 1
Localizer	RC-103	Provides lateral guidance.	Pilot	May be switched to any of following channels: U-108.3MC V-108.7MC W-109.1MC X-109.5MC Y-109.9MC Z-110.3MC	Fig. 4-5, Item 4.
Glide Path	AN/ARN-5	Provides vertical guidance.	(Turns on with the localizer switch.)		

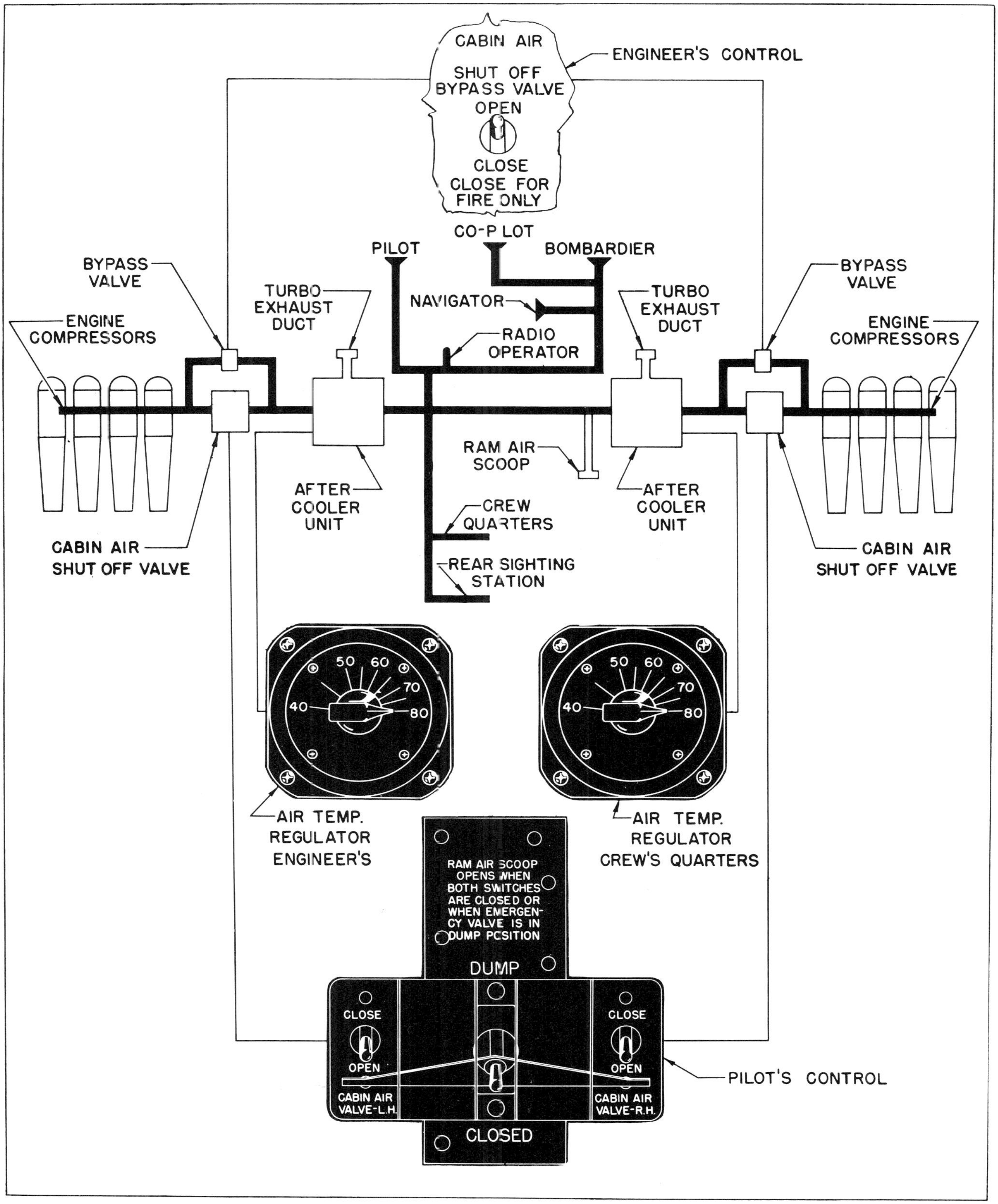

Figure 4-3. Heat, Vent, and Cabin Pressurizing System

4-23. GROUND CREW INTERPHONE SWITCH.- This switch is located on a panel below the engineer's instrument panel. (See 20 **figure** 1-12.) It has "ON" and "OFF" positions for connecting the ground crew jacks at the nose-wheel strut door into the interphone system.

4-24. RADIO COMPASS OPERATION.

a. Turn the jack box selector switch to "COMP." or plug the headset directly into the radio compass control box. The latter method disconnects the radio compass from the interphone system.

1. SUIT HEATER CONTROL BOX	8. RADIO JUNCTION BOX
2. OXYGEN REGULATOR	9. LIAISON DYNAMOTOR
3. INTERPHONE JACK BOX	10. INTERPHONE AMPLIFIER
4. ANTENNA REEL CONTROL BOX	11. COMMAND POWER JUNCTION BOX
5. LIAISON RECEIVER	12. COMMAND TRANSMITTER
6. ANTENNA CAPACITOR SWITCH (LIAISON)	13. COMMAND RECEIVER
7. LIAISON TRANSMITTER	14. LOW FREQUENCY RANGE RECEIVER

Figure 4-4. Radio Operator's Station

b. To start the radio compass, be sure the RADIO COMPASS and RADIO COMPASS AC switches on the radio junction box are switched on. To turn on the receiver, turn the function switch to either "COMP.", "ANT.", or "LOOP." Then push the "CONTROL" button to operate the green light indicating control from that station. The "COMP." position is used for automatic direction finding, the "ANT." position is used to listen to signals from the non-directional "sense" antenna, and in the "LOOP" position directional bearings are obtained on the compass indicator by manual control of the loop's rotation.

c. To stop the radio compass, turn the function switch "OFF."

4-25. LOW FREQUENCY RANGE RECEIVER OPERATION.

a. See that the SCR274 LOW FREQ. circuit breaker on the radio junction box is switched on. To turn on the receiver, place the "CW-OFF-MCW" switch on either "CW" or "MCW."

b. Plug the headset into the "A TEL." jack on the control box and place the "A-B" switch on "A."

NOTE

Both the radio compass and the low frequency set are connected at the same interphone switch position. If the radio compass is turned off, the pilot or any crew member may receive the low frequency output through the "COMP" position of his interphone jackbox.

c. Adjust the tuning dial and the "INCREASE OUTPUT" knob for best reception.

d. To turn the receiver off, move the "CW-OFF-MCW" switch to the "OFF" position.

4-26. COMMAND RADIO OPERATION.

a. See that the COMMAND RADIO circuit breaker on the radio junction box is switched on. To start the AN/ARC-3 radio, place the ON-OFF switch on the pilot's VHF COMMAND control panel in the "ON" position. Plug into any interphone jackbox and switch to "COMMAND."

b. Select the frequency channel by setting the eight-position selector switch at the desired position.

c. The pilot may transmit voice by actuating the press-to-talk switch on the control wheel, and speaking into the microphone. Code transmission may be effected by using the D/F TONE button on the control panel.

d. To receive, release the press-to-talk switch and the receiver will monitor the channel selected. Adjust the volume with the VOLUME control on the pilot's panel, or with the INCREASE OUTPUT knob on the jackbox.

e. All other crew members may transmit voice or receive through their interphone jackboxes, with the selector switch placed at the "COMMAND" position.

f. To stop the radio, turn the control switch "OFF."

4-27. LIAISON RECEIVER OPERATION.

a. See that the LIAISON RECEIVER circuit breaker on the radio junction box is switched on.

b. Plug the headset into the interphone jackbox and turn the selector switch to "LIAISON." The receiver controls are at the radio operator's station, and all other crew members may listen.

c. For modulated signal (voice) reception, turn the AVC-OFF-MVC switch to "MVC," turn the CW-OSC switch to "OFF," turn the CRYSTAL switch to "OUT," and set the BAND SWITCH and TUNING control to the desired frequency. Adjust the INCREASE VOL. control, or switch to "AVC," if desired, and then adjust the volume. Volume at jackboxes may be further reduced with the INCREASE OUTPUT knob.

d. For CW reception (code), proceed as for voice except turn the CW-OSC switch to "ON" and start with the BEAT FREQ. knob near the zero beat position (arrow on knob pointing up). Vary the BEAT FREQ. as desired, place the CRYSTAL switch in the "IN" position, and readjust the TUNING, BEAT FREQ., and INCREASE VOL. controls.

e. To stop the liaison receiver, turn the AVC-OFF-MVC switch to "OFF."

4-28. LIAISON TRANSMITTER OPERATION.

CAUTION

Under no circumstances should the transmitter be actually operating (key down or microphone switch closed) when the EMISSION switch is being operated. Such operation, especially at high altitudes, can cause an arc to occur and damage the contacts of relays.

a. The control box for releasing the trailing antenna and also a spare antenna are located to the left of the radio operator. See that the LIAISON TRANSMITTER circuit breaker on the radio junction box is switched on.

b. At the transmitter, set the LOCAL-REMOTE switch at "LOCAL," place the EMMISSION switch at "VOICE," and set the CHANNEL switch to the position corresponding to the frequency desired. When the red light comes on, set the EMISSION switch to the desired type of emission. Use the key or microphone as required by the type of emission chosen. Interphone jackboxes at the following crew stations are wired to permit voice transmission: radio operator, both pilots, and bombardier.

c. To stop the liaison transmitter, turn the EMISSION switch to the "OFF" position.

4-29. MARKER BEACON OPERATION.- The marker beacon receiver is connected into the radio compass control box so that any time the radio compass is in operation the marker beacon indicator light on the pilots' instrument panel indicates when the airplane is passing over a marker beacon transmitter.

4-30. IDENTIFICATION RADIO OPERATION.

a. Be sure the EMERGENCY switch on the pilot's identification radio panel is "OFF." Then switch on the "F" circuit breaker on the radio junction box and the 695 POWER switch on the control panel. Insert the destructor plug if necessary, but only if the red indicator lights are not burning.

b. For I-band operation, set the six-position coding switch on the selector control box to position "1" unless otherwise directed. Connect a headset into the power control box and listed for the characteristic switching noise.

c. Directions for use of all other parts of this equipment will be given by the communications officer-in-charge.

d. To stop the equipment, turn off the power switch and the "F" circuit breaker. Remove the destructor plug upon landing.

4-31. LOCALIZER AND GLIDE PATH RADIO OPERATION.

a. See that the LOCALIZER circuit breaker on the engineer's upper switch panel is switched on. Place the ON-OFF switch on the pilot's LOCALIZER panel in the "ON" position about 20 minutes before approaching the landing field.

b. Turn the channel selector switch to the desired position. Observe the course indications on the pilot's landing indicator.

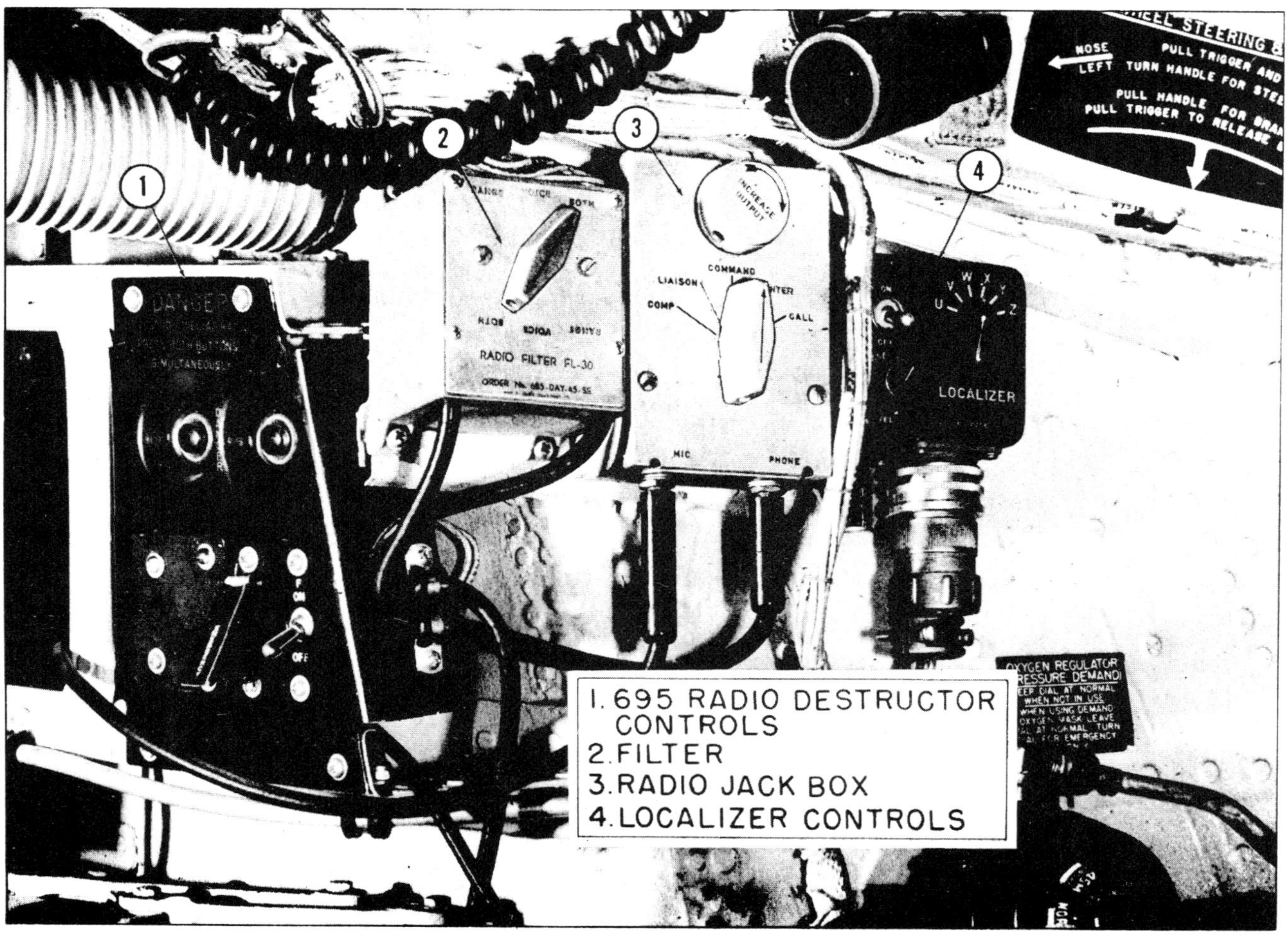

Figure 4-5. Pilot's Radio Controls

c. The audio output of the localizer receiver may be heard by plugging a headset into the pilot's control box, or through any interphone jackbox with the selector switch at the "COMMAND" position, if the command radio is not in operation. Volume may be adjusted by means of the INCREASE VOLUME control on the radio control box, which has no effect on the operation of the indicator.

4-32. GYRO FLUX GATE COMPASS.

4-33. GENERAL.

4-34. The master compass indicator is located on the navigator's instrument panel and a repeater indicator is installed on the pilots' instrument panel. All controls are located at the navigator's station, and the compass amplifier is located on the floor under the navigator's table. (See 5 and 7 figure 4-6.)

4-35. GYRO FLUX GATE COMPASS OPERATION.

a. Turn both the dc and ac switches "ON." Check to see that the amplifier switch is "ON."

b. Allow ten minutes after starting the gyro before caging or uncaging.

c. Erect the gyro by moving the toggle switch first to the "CAGE" position and then, after waiting a few seconds, to the "UNCAGED" position.

NOTE

Keep the toggle switch in the "UNCAGED" positions at all times except when running the caging cycle.

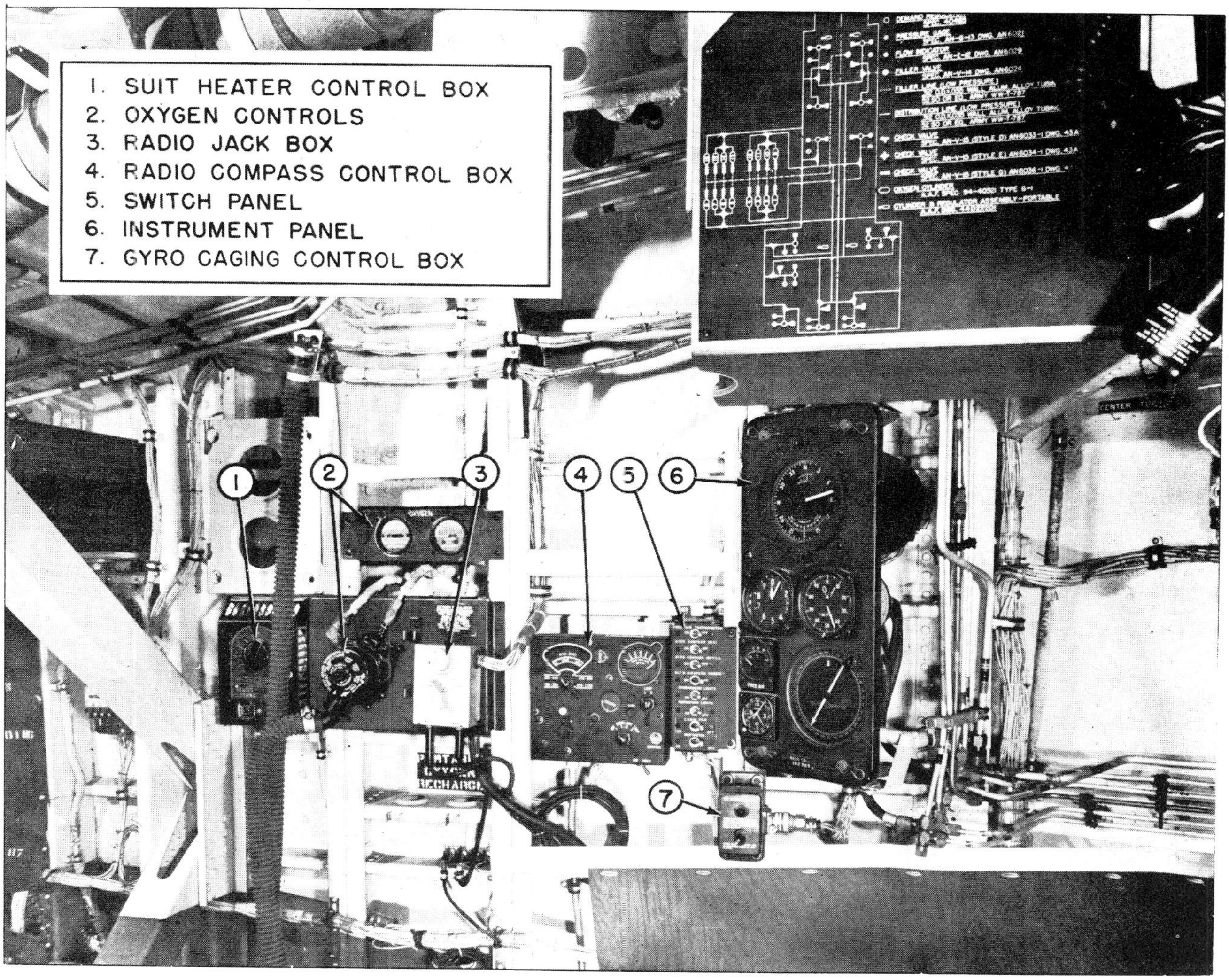

Figure 4-6. Navigator's Station

d. Correct the indicator for magnetic variation, if necessary.

e. Adjust the gain control on the amplifier.

f. To stop the gyro compass, turn the ac and dc switches "OFF."

4-36. DRIFT METER.

4-37. GENERAL.

4-38. The type B-3 gyro-stabilized drift meter is mounted at the outboard side of the navigator's seat. This particular model contains a starting transformer and push-button switch to enable the gyro to start and gain speed at extremely low temperatures. When this switch is depressed, the transformer momentarily impresses 220 volts into the electrical circuit, instead of the normal 110 volts ac.

4-39. DRIFT METER OPERATION.

a. Keep the gyro ON-OFF switch in the "OFF" position and the gyro caged when not in use.

b. See that the switch-type circuit breaker on the navigator's switch panel is turned "ON." (See 5 figure 4-6.) To start the drift meter, switch on the gyro and allow it to run for from three to five minutes before uncaging, Depress the push-button switch on the lower gyro housing for a maximum of one minute at the start of the starting procedure.

c. With the airplane in normal level flight, uncage the gyro by pulling out the caging knob and moving it to the uncaged position.

d. When sighting through the eyepiece, turn the rheostat knob to adjust the illumination of the reticle lines. If the ground image is too bright, interpose the shade glass by means of the lever on the filter housing.

e. Adjust the focus of the eyepiece, by operation of the ocular housing holder on the upper gyro housing, until the reticle lines are sharp and clear.

Figure 4-7. SCR 274 Radio Controls (On Pilots' Pedestal)

f. To stop the equipment, cage the gyro by pulling out the caging knob and moving it as far as possible toward the caged position. Turn the gyro switch "OFF" and turn off the reticle lamp.

4-40. BOMBING EQUIPMENT.

4-41. GENERAL.

4-42. There are three bomb bays in each wing, numbered from two to four in the left wing and five to seven in the right wing. Each bomb bay is equipped with a flexible door. The doors roll onto drums at the aft end of the bays when they are opened. The all-electric bomb release and indicator light systems are based on AAF standard systems. The bomb control panel is located on the nacelle wall to the bombardier's right. (See figure 4-8.) A type B3-A bomb release interval control is used to control the release of bombs. A standard "press-to-release bomb switch, on a flexible cord, extends from the aft side of the control panel. (See 5 figure 4-8.)

4-43. BOMBING CONTROLS.

4-44. BOMB RELEASE INTERVAL CONTROLS.

4-45. TRAIN SELECTOR SWITCH.- This switch is used to select either train release of bombs, or, using a separate operation of the bomb release switch, selective bomb release. The switch has two positions, "TRAIN" and "SEL." If for any reason it is desired to stop a train of bombs before the total number selected has been released, moving this switch to "SEL." will immediately stop the bomb release.

4-46. COUNTER SWITCH.- The counter switch is a rotary switch which is used to select the number of bombs to be dropped in train. As bombs are being dropped, from one to fifty can be selected and, if desired to drop more than originally selected or more than fifty, the switch can be held manually at any point above zero. Turning the selector switch to zero at any time will automatically stop the release of bombs. The switch must be set at least one minute before release of bombs.

4-47. INTERVAL SELECTOR DIAL.- The interval selector dial regulates the spacing in feet, relative to ground speed, of the bombs dropped in train.

4-48. BOMB RELEASE INDICATOR LIGHT.- This light is situated below the counter switch. It is used to indicate that the interval control has been prepared for release of bombs or that the selector switch is on selective release, and pressure on the bomb release switch will release a bomb or bombs.

4-49. BOMBARDIER'S POWER SUPPLY SWITCH.- This switch, located in the lower forward corner of the bombardier's control panel, opens or closed the electrical power supply to the bombing control systems. When the

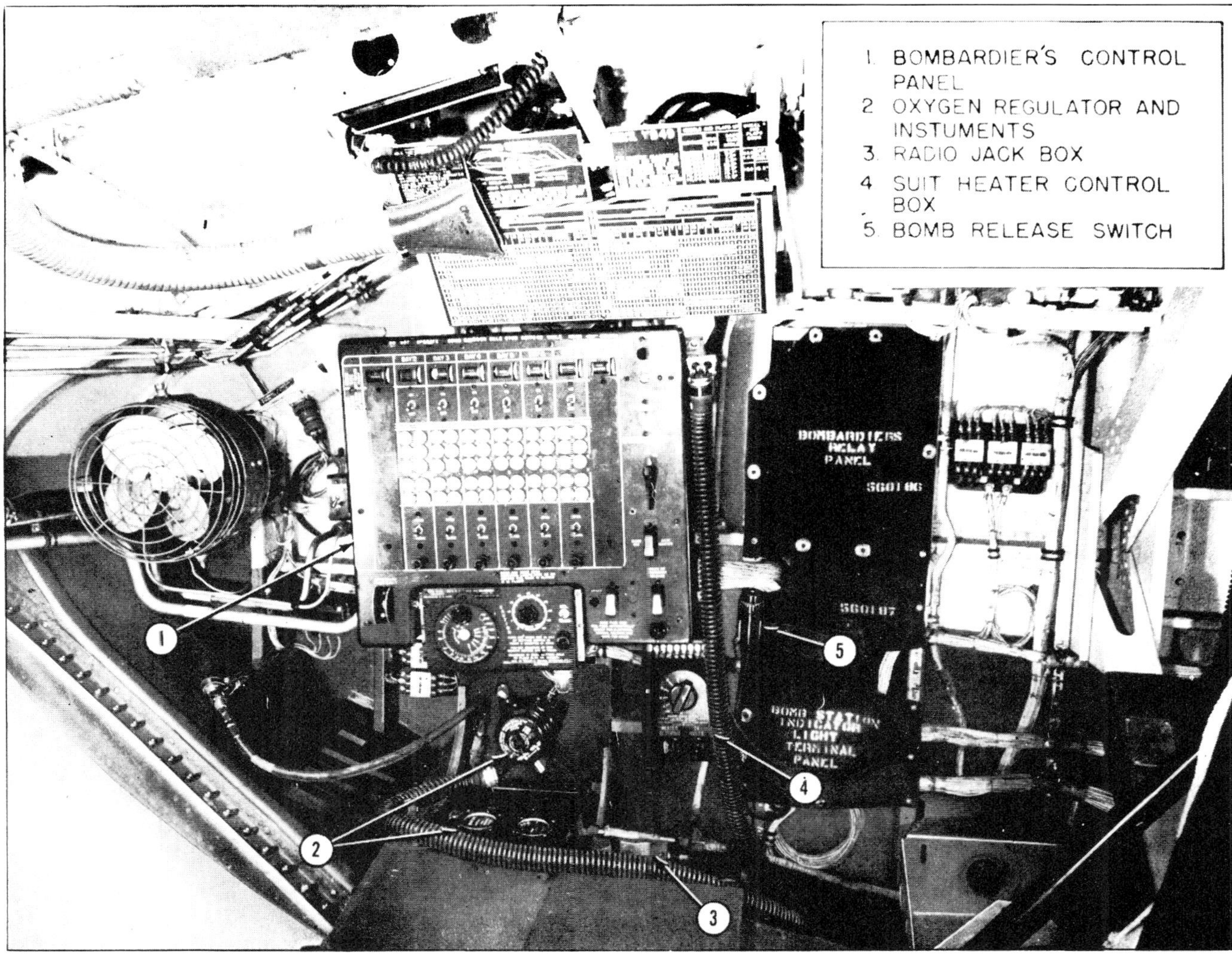

Figure 4-8. Bombardier's Station

airplane is on the ground, this switch should be left in the "OFF" position to prevent inadvertent operation of the bomb bay doors.

4-50. BOMB SALVO SWITCHES AND INDICATOR LIGHTS.- A bomb salvo switch and indicator light is located on the bombardier's control panel, at the pilot's station, and two switches and lights are installed next to the escape hatch into No. 4 bomb bay. The switch at the aft side of the escape hatch, the pilot's, and the bombardier's salvo switches will open all bomb bay doors and drop all bombs in a "safe" condition. The switch at the forward side of the escape will open and release the bombs "safe" from No. 4 bomb bay only.

4-51. NOSE-FUSE ARMING SWITCH AND INDICATOR LIGHT.- This switch is located next to the interval controls. When the switch is in the "ARMED" position the indicator light will be on. The light is a conventional push-to-test light.

NOTE

Tail fuse is automatically armed for normal electrical release and "safe" for salvo release.

4-52. BOMB BAY DOOR MASTER SWITCH.- This switch is protected by a guard and when in the "ON" position it will operate the bomb bay doors selected by the BOMB BAY DOOR INDICATOR AND SELECTOR SWITCHES.

4-53. BOMB BAY DOOR INDICATOR LIGHTS AND SELECTOR SWITCHES.- Each bomb bay door is provided with a two-position switch and an indicator light for the open position of the door. When any of these switches is moved to the "OPEN" or "CLOSE" position and the BOMB BAY DOOR MASTER switch is turned "ON," the corresponding doors will move to the selected position. These switches must be selected to correspond with the BOMB BAY SELECTOR SWITCH positions.

4-54. BOMB BAY SELECTOR SWITCHES.- These selector switches control the power to their respective bomb release systems. They and the bomb bay door selector switches must be operated together in pairs for selective release in the following order: Bomb bays 2 and 7, 3 and 6, and 4 and 5.

NOTE

As long as the auxiliary power units are installed in bomb bays three and six, and the A.P.U. fuel tanks in bomb bay five, these three bays contain no bombing equipment which is wired for operation.

4-55. BOMB STATION INDICATOR LIGHTS AND CONTROL SWITCHES.- An indicator for each bomb station is located on the control panel. An INDICATOR LIGHTS test switch is installed on the control panel. When held to the "TEST" position, with ac power available, all lights should illuminate. The indicator light switch located below the test switch is for the purpose of determining the loaded bomb stations. When this switch is turned "ON" one indicator light will show for each loaded bomb station. The power supply switch must be on to make this check.

4-56. BOMB SIZE LOAD INDICATORS.- These indicators can be turned by means of a knurled wheel adjacent to each indicator. Before flight these indicators should be turned to show the size bomb carried in the respective bomb bay.

4-57. BOMBING SYSTEM OPERATION.

a. Select the desired bomb bays by placing the BOMB BAY SELECTOR switches in the "ON" position and the corresponding BOMB BAY DOOR INDICATOR AND SELECTOR switches in the "OPEN" position.

CAUTION

These switches must be operated in pairs according to the firing order. See paragraph 4-54.

c. Test the indicator lights by holding the INDICATOR LIGHT TEST switch to the "TEST" position.

d. Set the interval control to "SEL" or "TRAIN." If train release is desired, adjust the control dials as necessary.

e. To open the bomb bay doors, move the BOMB BAY DOOR MASTER switch to the "ON" position.

CAUTION

Do not attempt to change the direction of door movement while they are moving. Damage to the door operating mechanism will result.

f. If nose arming is desired, move the nose fuse arming switch to the "ARMED" position.

g. To check the loaded bomb stations, move the INDICATOR LIGHT switch to the "ON" position. Be sure to return this switch to the "OFF" position, as bombs cannot be released tail armed while the switch is "ON."

h. If bombs are to be released in train, press and release the bomb switch. For selective release, press and release the switch for each bomb dropped.

NOTE

Train release may be stopped by turning the interval control to "O."

i. Close the bomb bay doors by placing the BOMB BAY DOOR INDICATOR AND SELECTOR switches in the "CLOSE" position and then move the master door switch to the "ON" position. When the doors have completed their movement, move the master door switch to the "OFF" position.

4-58. LIGHTING EQUIPMENT.

4-59. EXTERIOR LIGHTS.

4-60. LANDING LIGHT SWITCHES. (See 7 figure 1-30.)- Two switches are used to operate the landing lights. One switch is used to extend and retract the lights and the other is used to turn them on and off.

4-61. POSITION AND FORMATION LIGHT SWITCHES. (See 8 figure 1-30.)- Three switches are provided for these lights: one for the wing lights, one for the tail lights and one for the formation lights. The switches have "BRIGHT-OFF-DIM" positions.

4-62. INTERIOR LIGHTS.

4-63. LIGHTING CHART.

TYPE AND LOCATION	NO. OF LIGHTS	SWITCH LOCATION
DOME LIGHTS. Flight crew's compartment and crew's quarters.	3 fwd. 2 aft	On light panel.
EXTENSION LIGHTS. Above bombardier's, engineer's, and radio operator's stations.	3	On light panel.

TYPE AND LOCATION	NO. OF LIGHTS	SWITCH LOCATION
COCKPIT LIGHTS. At each flight crew station and aft gunner's station.	9	*Rear of lamp housing.
FLUORESCENT COCKPIT LIGHTS. Pilots' station (6), bombardier's station (1), navigator's station (2), engineer's station (7), radio operator's station (2), aft gunner's station (1).	19	*Rear of lamp housing.
TABLE LIGHT. Navigator's station.	1	Navigator's switch panel.

*Engineer's lights also have switch-type circuit breakers on the lower elect. control panel. (See figure 1-26.)

4-64. CABIN FANS.

4-65. FAN AND SWITCH LOCATIONS.

4-66. Four electric fans are installed in the crew nacelle for ventilating purposes located as follows: one directly behind the pilot, one near the engineer's station, one at the bombardier station and one in the crew's quarters. A switch-type circuit breaker on the navigator's switch panel operates the fan at the bombardier's station. Switches are provided adjacent to the other three fans. A switch-type circuit breaker is located on the engineer's upper electrical control panel for these three fans.

PILOT'S NOTES